What's the Problem Now?

Black Grievances and White Guilt

What's the Problem Now?

Black Grievances and White Guilt

Michael Brandow

Published by New English Review Press
a subsidiary of World Encounter Institute
PO Box 158397
Nashville, Tennessee 37215
&
27 Old Gloucester Street
London, England, WC1N 3AX

Cover Art and Design by Kendra Mallock

ISBN: 978-1-943003-84-6

Library of Congress Control Number: 2023934906

First Edition

NEW ENGLISH REVIEW PRESS
newenglishreview.org

CONTENTS

CULTURE CLASH

I am so bored with black people.

One morning, a few summers ago, I was seated alone and enjoying breakfast in my favorite Montreal coffee shop, a busy, crowded place with good food, great prices, and no attitude. Face down and deep in thought over a local paper, I noticed a new presence beside me. Without looking up, relying on that uncanny faculty of peripheral vision with which we humans of all genders, races, colors, and creeds have been blessed, I could make out a couple, a man and a woman (not that gender is relevant here), both black (for whatever that's worth), standing next to my tiny, wobbly table, silently waiting for me to make room so they could pass and sit at the next.

The woman slipped informally around the front of my table and took a seat by the wall, but the man stood there to my left, not saying a word. I did what I would've done for anyone, regardless of gender, race, color, or creed, seeking passage with, or even without so much as an "Excuse me, please. Could I get by?" I stayed seated and simply pushed my chair forward, stomach pressed uncomfortably against the table's edge, and continued reading. I took a bite of my poutine omelette, a local specialty, then sipped my coffee, hoping to breathe normally again once the man had joined his woman friend to look at the menu.

He just stood there, as though waiting for something. He had a kind of firm resolve to his stance, I sensed inexplicably without looking up, the sort I'd seen in photos of passive resisters during civil rights protests in streets of the Deep South back in the sixties. Apparently, my gesture of accommodation wasn't enough for the stranger, who just happened to be black. Had I not made room enough for him, or any other normal person, to get by? Was I missing something?

I finally glanced up from my reading. No one else in the restaurant seemed to have noticed the couple, let alone cared they were black, the only black people there that morning. Diners went on chatting and eating and sipping their coffee. Only the waiter, part of his job being crowd control, saw the man while passing hurriedly, a plate balancing on each hand. This was a small place. It was rush hour. He quickly sized up the situation, and quite without ceremony said: "There's enough room." The man taking up space seemed also to want our time and attention, but compliantly he passed, without effort or fanfare, via the generous corridor I'd created behind my chair. He took his place opposite the woman at the next table and let me breathe easily again.

"You need help with that, too?" I was glad not to have said when reflecting, later that day, on this tense little encounter. I'd wanted nothing that morning but to be left in peace to have my breakfast and read my paper, not to be drawn into a contrived racial confrontation or make some pointless political point. They might as well have been carrying signs. The woman, as a matter of fact, had "BLACK GIRL" scrawled loudly in bold capital letters across her T-shirt, in case anyone didn't notice. "We have just enough time to eat before my lecture," she said in a thick southern accent while perusing the menu, raising her voice on that last word. Still no reaction from the crowd that went on chatting and sipping, though Canadians do tend to eat this stuff up. Obviously, one of the local universities cared enough about this black girl to invite her to speak. A chance to hear how badly we treat her people south of the border? And from a genuine oppressed black come all this way from the American South to testify? Who could resist?

Canadians like to blame Americans for everything under the sun, from racism, to global warming, to currents in the Saint Lawrence River. In fact much of their national identity is derived, not so much from what they *are* as from what they say they are *not*: Americans. Self-styled Dudley Do-Rights, compared to those bad folks beneath them, blameless babes in the northern woods, Canadians call themselves "the world's peacekeepers," an easy job when you're perched on the back

of a superpower with concerns a bit more compli-
cated than yours. Unlike Americans, it should be
said, Canadians do take care of their own, more or
less, with universal health care and other goodies.
But the whole enterprise only stays afloat because
Canada is a rich, fat country with a surplus economy based on getting their hands dirty with oil,
oil extracted in the filthiest possible way possible,
from tar sands. Our holier-than-thou neighbors
also shame us for slavery and its aftermath, ignor-
ing their own genocidal history, not to mention
the many family skeletons in their ancestral Eu-
ropean closets. Somehow they manage to avoid
reading a wealth of current studies and reports,
some from their own government, on widespread
"racialized poverty" in Canada today. Instead, they
migrate like geese to favorite vacation spots, poor
places like Mexico and India, many Canadians I've
known staying for months or years at a time. They
land like beneficent aliens, dropping their *sous* for
grateful peasants who would otherwise, the condescending Canadians tell themselves, have none.
They exploit these faraway, exotic cultures with
their strong currency, take advantage of local
markets for slave labor—then return home feel-

ing more virtuous than Americans than they did before.

But enough of Canadian transparency. Returning to something the new activists have been calling "visibility," I'm still perplexed over what, exactly, that black American man in a Montreal diner was expecting of me that morning several summers ago. Some sort of formal recognition of his presence? Some grandiose gesture? A heartfelt apology for slavery? Perhaps I could have been more sensitive and less dismissive by lifting my eyes from the article I was reading, rising above my pride and stepping aside, maybe bowing as he passed and my eggs got cold? This all seemed a bit overdone. It wasn't like anyone was asking this couple to step to the rear, just to step around, as anyone else in the restaurant that day would've done without feeling in the least bit slighted, or being, as the activists also say, "marginalized," the opposite of having "visibility."

Returning home to New York City, where daily life isn't quite as simple as in Canada, I realized why I'd nearly said something that could have led to an argument, or worse. It was because I'd been dealing with these irritating social snafus, these "microaggressions," as the activists say, a lot in recent years, and I was hoping to take a break from them while on vacation in the Great White North (emphasis on "white"). Everywhere I went in New York, it was seeming harder all the time to avoid some unpleasant clash with a touchy total stranger, to get through my day without inadvertently stepping on black toes, or on the white toes of self-appointed Emily Posts speaking for the "historically oppressed." A growing body of nitpicky rules, and the constant likelihood of committing some innocent infraction, made for much tiptoeing. Whether on the subway or sidewalk, in parks, restaurants or shops, the "socially cognizant," as the activists call repentant whites like themselves, bend over backwards to enforce the latest rules of etiquette, watching for hidden landmines and in a perpetual state of hyper-vigilance lest they, too, slip up and offend the hyper-sensitive who seem to understand our culture no better than I do theirs.

I don't like to generalize but: Why do so many black people I encounter go to such elaborate lengths to ride the latest white guilt trip—if not to make compliant Caucasians jump through their demanding hoops? A couple years before the restaurant incident, just downstairs from my Greenwich Village apartment, trouble was brewing in the supermarket I'd been shopping for a half-century without incident. I noticed the launching of a strange new custom, one I'd never known to exist in either white or black culture, an experiment being tested on unwitting whites.

A group of black girls who worked as cashiers at the supermarket were demanding, apparently on their own initiative and with no direction from management or corporate headquarters, to be paid in a new way. Rather than count cash on the counter and leave it there for them to collect, as I'd always done, I was being told to hand it over directly into the black cashiers' hands. No other form of cash payment, as far as they were concerned, would be socially acceptable. If I erred and regressed into my old ways, I was told "That's *rude*. You need to hand it to me." This was news to me. Never lay the money down? I wondered what the black croupiers I'd seen in Atlantic City, or the black bank tellers working just down the block, would say to having cash placed directly into their hands.

I do, it turns out, "need to hand it to" those black-girl cashiers. For a time, most of the white customers in this very white neighborhood complied with their categorical demand, not polite request, giving them the benefit of the doubt about some vital aspect of black culture they must have missed, some painful part of "the black experience," as my agonizingly tolerant neighbors called it, yet to be revealed. Meanwhile, cynics like me rolled our eyes while doing as told, risking not only the "rude" label, but that other *r* word. I knew it was the public scolding many feared. It was that big, fat finger of Aunt Jemima, whose familiar face still graced those supermarket shelves, that worried whities didn't want waving in their faces for all to see, her other hand planted firmly on her hip in a determined "mammy" stance.

One day I forgot about the new house rule and left my money on the counter. The black girl stood and stared with widened, vaudevillian eyes, unable to believe my arrogance but eager to close the trap she had laid.

"Pick it up!" she shouted, alerting her fellow cashiers whose jaws dropped at my audacity.

"No, *you* pick it up," I answered calmly, trying

to call her bluff by leaving my two twenty-dollar bills flatly on the counter without apology.

"I am not picking that up. You are rude!" she cried, about to apply, I was certain, that other *r* word.

"Now give me my change and stop acting silly," I said.

"Pick it up!"

"No, you pick it up," I answered calmly again, stoking her anger to a cartoonish extreme.

We went back and forth like this for a minute or so, the black girl's voice rising each time I responded quietly, almost inaudibly. The two twenty-dollar bills lay there uncollected, and a line formed behind me. The black girl, enraged at this point, left her post in a huff to get the manager.

"He won't pick this up," she told the black man who'd managed the place for years, who was on friendly terms with me and not as sympathetic to her struggle as she'd predicted.

"Pick it up," he told the cashier with that same blunt lack of ceremony as the Quebecois waiter who told the indignant black man, in so many words, to cut the bullshit and sit his ass down. The activist complied silently and I left with my change and groceries. The rebel gang of black girls never bothered anyone again for leaving money on the counter. Their activism had backfired, at least this time. As for me, I'd managed, single-handedly, to win a small battle in the culture war. I'd aborted the birth of yet another arbitrary piece of political correctness, this one in the very making, another needless formality with a purpose obvious to no one but me, before it could spread beyond that supermarket and become the new normal.

One thing the new activists don't understand—or do they?—is that daily life in a large, multicultural metropolis is full of broken rules and dashed expectations. Here in New York City, we have a rich and vibrant mix of Koreans and Germans, Afghans and Algerians, West Africans and Northern Irish, people from everywhere in the world sharing the same spaces and doing this remarkably well. Not to dismiss chances for misunderstandings—but why go out of the way to manufacture more? Years have passed since the supermarket incident, and still I've learned of no law of etiquette in black American culture, or in native African cultures, requiring shoppers to place money directly into the hand of a cashier, rather than count and leave it on the counter to be recounted and placed in the till. These black girls clearly had some hidden agenda, some point to make. Sadly for everyone black, white, or whatever, the matter hasn't ended there. My supermarket story, like my restaurant story, are symptoms of an antisocial disease seeping into every aspect of daily life, and not just in New York. Situations vary, but the story is always the same: If you can't find enough reasons to feel marginalized and oppressed, and to shame people for marginalizing and oppressing you—*then just make shit up!*

Disingenuous bids for "visibility" are by no means isolated events, but part of a broader trend to spotlight, not only some overblown racial identity, but a perceived gender. Why, for example, would affluent, over-educated white people (who compose the vast majority of "woke" folk on the planet) want to add to an ever-expanding list of imaginary "gender identities" invented from thin air, and then to an endless roster of bizarre corresponding "pronouns" made up to match—if not to contrive yet another reason for being offended? Because, on some level, they understand the dynamic and how to work it. If you truly do "know your own truth," as the aggrieved like to say, then you are by definition special, marginal—perceived genders multiply so militantly, you might very well be the only person on the planet knowing this particular truth!—but you need not be ignored. As a "gender nonconforming" activist, you can metamorphose into both an annoying gadfly, and a wandering flytrap for "bigots" blind to your uniqueness, and ignorant of the neologisms you coined just yesterday. The ultimate goal of these exercises, performed as in spin classes by members of society's elite who can never seem to get enough "visibility," is to show that they, too, and despite their vast privilege and media presence, feel invisible, just like black people do, that they feel their pain, understand their struggle, and join their fight. Just as soon as they've finished their champagne brunches in restaurants where they would eagerly be seen taking a knee for any passing black man, if only they could find one who could afford to dine where they do.

All this making and enforcing of intricate social rules, this catering to the easily miffed, might seem, if only to an unrefined boor like myself, the activities of idle minds, obsessions of the pathologically self-indulgent. This growing fad for propriety rewards compliance and has concerns as petty as the punishments—public shaming, ostracism, career casualties—are harsh. Call me a racist, as I'm sure many will in these times of heightened alert to choosing one's words carefully, but about the only confession I'd ever make to the uptight mob is to still, in all honesty, not understand what makes a "person of color" so very different from a "colored person." Does world peace hinge on a preposition? Guilty as charged of being indelicate, I've always made light of correctness, political or otherwise, though I do understand that while many black people unknowingly take their cues from the decadent whites who control the schools and media, in black culture, the slightest breach of decorum can get a person more than shunned: It can get you shot.

Meanwhile, elevated and above it all, safe from contradiction in their rarified atmosphere of right and wrong, wealthy, white "social justice warriors," either young or trying to recapture their youths with radicalism, by the passion and scale of their campaign to prescribe every aspect of daily life, manage to put to shame even those old Victorians who wrote the etiquette manuals for social climbers terrified of offending society's sensibilities. Perhaps a generation that lives on Twitter, a tight-assed, corseted culture where an affront to *bienséance* is grounds for exile and disgrace, wants to make the world more like Twitter? There, the virtually virtuous are encouraged to know their own truths, but any step beyond the straight-and-narrow list of acceptable truths can be a socially-fatal *faux pas*.

And yet despite the virtual traps and false indignation of recent years, there are, always have been, genuine cultural clashes based on ignorance or insensitivity, lapses that might accurately be called "problematic," however grossly overused and boring this word has become. Over my many years of getting around in New York City, the ultimate melting pot where tensions can sometimes be high, I know from vast experience one perennial point of contention between blacks and whites, not around race or gender, but around another species altogether: dogs.

Call me a racist, if you haven't already, this time for making the observation that black people tend not to feel about dogs as many white people do. Socio-economics and disposable income aside, dogs have always had different meanings in different cultures. Sometimes they're loved, pampered, worshipped. Sometimes they're dinner. I remember one of my anthropology professors back in college using an expression, "the dog of house," to distinguish the interspecies affections of people like me from those who would never, not under any circumstances, have humans and hounds living under the same roof.

Or sharing the same sidewalk. I've tried, unsuccessfully over my many years of walking dogs for a living in New York City, to withhold judgment, to delay my knee-jerk reactions to blacks immersing themselves in my culture but not caring to respect just what dogs mean to white people like me. "Do as the Romans do"? Fat chance. Black culture may be mere miles or even blocks away, but a world separates us, and further divides us each time—enough times over a lifetime to establish a pattern—I'm walking my dogs and approached from behind by a black girl with an angry:

"*Excuse* me!"

Now, if I were plagued with white guilt, as today's frightened yet self-righteous white folks are, I might feel grateful for getting more consideration from an irate black girl than I got from that black guy in the restaurant who stood silently, smugly, waiting for me to figure out just what he expected. The expectation in these sidewalk situations is clear, but it's the unmistakable tone of sarcasm in that *"Excuse* me!" that colors an otherwise polite request aimed at me and my best friends. These brusque encounters almost always begin from behind, fully beyond the scope of my peripheral vision, so they're obviously not about stepping aside to make room for a passerby, but the very fact of letting dogs take up sidewalk space at all. This is what my black critics—almost all of them Nubian princesses, for some reason—resent, or at least pretend to find offensive while wandering insensitively around my culture and expecting us locals to accommodate *them*, not the other way around.

The white gloves come off and any pretension to politeness is dropped by the curbside when they skip the *"Excuse* me!" and go straight for: "Git dem dam dawgz out da way!" Either way, these unpleasant and unnecessary dog-hating episodes are by no means isolated events. Based on my own personal "lived experience," as the new leftists say, and on statistics, not only anti-dog hate crimes, but anti-white, anti-gay, anti-Asian, and anti-Jewish hate crimes in my culture are disproportionately committed by the same "historically oppressed"[1] people. Still I strive to conquer my cultural myopia by returning to my studies in anthropology and making—if they won't—a counterintuitive case for patience and understanding. These angry black girls on a mission, the ones who always approach with the same words in the same sarcastic tone, and almost always from behind, are very likely afraid of dogs. Fear does ugly things to people. Dogs, I try and remember, don't tend to be beloved companions and family members in their culture, but rather tools for protection, intimidation, drug running. Dogs, in black American culture, are pit bulls.

The only problem with my noble attempt at tolerance is, the dogs I tend to walk are every type *but* pit bull. And why do these tiffs always involve a black girl, a hefty one at that, and not a black man? I can only guess that, like those co-conspirator cashiers in the supermarket, these girls have been talking and they know how to get under a white person's skin. Once again, their clever plan backfires when they stumble on some unaccommodating cracker like myself. Coming to my culture to throw your weight around is bad enough. Attack my dogs, even if you "know your own truth," and you have crossed a line.

"If you don't like dogs, then what the fuck are you doing in the Village?" is my standard reply once I've awoken from my brief "woke" dream of tolerance and accommodation to the smell of black coffee.

"Why don't you try losing some weight off that fat ass?" I continue, careful not to add "black" and risk arrest for hate speech. The obese black girl's eyes grow vaudevillian at the sight of a white person who won't roll over submissively, tail between his legs, for a tummy scratch and a pardon.

"Make some room for the rest of us, why don't you?" I add to drive my point home.

Knowing she's met her match, she waddles around us with her enormous carcass, unobstructed and hardly inconvenienced, as she easily could have done without starting an argument in the first place. Her behind now fully "visible" to me, having called so much attention to herself, she storms off in a huff, sometimes threatening to send one of her homies to teach me some manners.

Am I being a biased, culturally insensitive slob—or is the loud, pushy black girl? Do I dwell upon minute "microaggressions" against me while ignorant of more pervasive "systemic," "structural," and "unconscious" forces at work against blacks? I think not. Having read much of the academic "theory" and heard its preachers, I'm still forced to conclude that avoidable resentment, fear, and yes, racial boredom are born, not of sinister, unseen forces holding down black people, but of these very mundane sidewalk snits that get started, every time, by black people. To be sure, the high-minded, sciency-sounding terms enshrined in universities are parroted by mainstream media, then inserted into sidewalk shout downs to lend a veneer of legitimacy, an air of erudition to the black girls' grievances. But rest assured, there is nothing "unconscious" about my *ennui* with that enormous walrus who once approached me, and mine, head-on along a stretch of sidewalk off Seventh Avenue more than broad enough to fit, comfortably, both her fat ass and any number of dogs I might have been walking. She picked up speed, as best she could with a hanging mass of flesh and black skin, the fruit of many trips to Popeyes. She plowed straight toward us, forcing me to pull my four small, fragile pups narrowly but safely out of harm's way, out of her chosen path to "visibility." Call me a racist, once again, but these moments leave lasting imprints that all the academic theory in the world won't erase.

Am I overreacting? On the contrary, based on my decades of experience walking dogs and dealing with passersby, I can safely say that the reactions from big black girls to my animals taking up public space are a kind of barometer for the current state of race relations in this country.

One day, the latest viral video shows, on YouTube and out of context, police shooting the latest career criminal to have just been resisting arrest, attacking officers, maybe stealing their weapons—and my dogs and I get nothing but grief from those hefty heifers promenading the Village to show me how mad they are.

But after thousands of sympathetic white "woke" folks take to the streets and burn things, the black girls, the same ones who'd just as soon trample over my pups, suddenly can't resist stepping aside and saying, in high-pitched baby talk, how "cute" they are.

If the police officers involved in the shooting of another unarmed black man, including any "self-loathing" black police officers also involved, avoid jail time for doing their jobs, we're back to a nasty "*Excuse* me!" again.

The cops who shot the violent career criminal are fired, maybe given prison time, and the sidewalks are lovey-dovey again.

Call me a racist—at this point I can live with that—but I am bored with the black girls who, after plowing through my culture like pit bulls in a china shop, suddenly want to show me their softer, nurturing sides when it suits them.

On the other hand, some black people may not necessarily be offended at all by my having dogs on the sidewalk, whatever the current state of race relations, provided I have the right dogs. Visiting my culture from near and far, they don't seem to mind the dachshunds, a breed to which blacks seem universally partial. What makes dachsies so exceptional to dog haters? I suppose it's the extreme deformities that make these cartoon critters seem nonthreatening to outsiders normally afraid of dogs. The small stature, freakishly long backs, and severely shortened, stumpy legs make these poor mutants seem barely able to walk, much less to hurt a black person.

Little do the dachsie exceptionalists know, they're about to rush up and pet, without asking permission, a breed that studies and reports reveal to be not always so sweet and cuddly, but among the more aggressive breeds, a top biter in the U.S., right up there with pit bulls!

I might stop and explain this to the black girl who graciously approves of my dogs, so long as they're of the right 'race.' Too late. She reaches so fast to pet that I have no choice but to add her to my list of tourists who bumble naively through my culture, only to learn, the hard way, the danger in judging by appearances.

ENDNOTES

1 Post Editorial Board, "Who commits hate crimes and other commentary," *New York Post*, May 24, 2022, https://nypost.com/2022/05/24/who-commits-hate-crimes-and-other-commentary/.

two

WHITE PEOPLE BEING BLACK

I was still a bit shaken that evening when a friend called to give me news of the next exotic vacation she and her boyfriend were planning. I tried to sound interested, but the distraction of what had just happened, or what might have happened had I been less lucky, was almost too much to bear without telling someone, if only the police.

Minutes earlier, I was approaching my apartment building, carrying two grocery bags and fumbling for my keys. I cut diagonally across

West Fourth Street, heavy with traffic day and night, weaved through the pileup of honking cars, and stepped up the curb and onto the sidewalk, mobbed as usual with passersby. The crowd on my block is especially thick after six at night, and crossing those final few feet to my front door can be a challenge. I balanced on the curb with grocery bags in both arms, preparing to dart across and timing my trajectory to miss the many moving bodies that passed, then seamlessly take flight upstairs to end a hard day and make dinner. A seasoned pro at navigating the city, I scouted out the first clearing, readied to rush out, lean against the door, and insert the key, in my hand long before I'd even crossed West Fourth, then close the door behind me, in case of another encounter like the night before …

The night before, I'd barely turned the key to my front door, and a black girl pushed me in from behind, sandwiching us both in the small vestibule where the mailboxes are. I could see from the corner of an eye that, unlike the many walruses with whom I'd had run-ins from behind, she was slim, wearing what looked like a business suit, and was quite pretty.

"I got a *phagina* for sale," she said in an up-beat tone, not unlike a door-to-door encyclopedia salesman trying to make something dull sound sexy. Did she know the chances of stumbling on a gay guy in Greenwich Village? Her naïveté was endearing.

"I got a *phagina* for sale," she repeated, in case I hadn't heard. I turned around, looked her straight in the eye, and said in a bald-faced appropriation of black English:

"Sorry, but you barkin' up *da wrong tree*, honey!"

I felt embarrassed for this enterprising black girl. She was a real mover-and-shaker, unafraid to move in on a potential sale and do some shakin'. But she knew how to cut her losses with a gay guy in the Village. Having received my message loudly and clearly, she turned and ran back into the crowd to find some taker for her "*phagina.*" What I got from this cross-cultural exchange was a funny story to tell people for years to come. What I almost got on the night of that other culture clash, just before my friend called with her travel plans, wasn't funny at all.

"Hey don't you cut in frunna me like dat, you

white ole asshole!" screamed a tall, muscular black guy who didn't have love for sale.

"You rude mothafucka! I cut yo ass!" he elaborated as I struggled to get my key into the lock before he could maybe get a knife into *moi*. Somehow, crossing the sidewalk to get home and make dinner, I had committed some unconscious racial transgression against a black man in whose culture, likely mere miles or even blocks away, they had different rules for respecting personal space. This was odd, I thought in that split second as the door opened and my life flashed before me, because I'd crossed the sidewalk a good six feet away from him. He could very well have kept walking, unimpeded and unoffended, but chose instead to stop in his tracks, take a moment from his busy day, and make some sort of political point about being cut short, "marginalized," or robbed of "visibility," high-minded terms he might have parroted from the academics but not the words he chose to express his rage.

"Fuckin' rude-ass fuckin' white-ass ole mothafucka!" he added for emphasis. Whatever had I done to offend this man? Perhaps I should have stepped aside and taken a knee, as I might have done for that black man in the Montreal coffee shop, issuing a heartfelt apology for that slavery thing as he passed? Though convinced I had the right of way, having crossed in front of him a good six feet ahead, I'd been dealing with these high-adrenaline sidewalk situations for almost a half-century and had no interest in reasoning with another angry black man who was in no mood for diplomacy. I kept silent, focusing on the survival task at hand, slipping through the door and slamming it shut before he could follow. His muffled screams of outrage, I was sure, spoke centuries of oppression. They followed me up five flights and into my apartment where I bolted the door and the phone rang.

"Yeah, it must be that slavery thing he's so riled about," I snickered to myself before taking the call from a friend more "socially cognizant" than I, a person unlikely to appreciate the dark humor in my latest story. I had so many. Tired after yet another hard day of dodging offended black people and ready for a cocktail, I decided not to bother telling her about my latest culture clash. It only would have led to another argument.

My friend was brimming with excitement

over the trip she and her boyfriend, like so many of their generation, were planning. As the millennium came to a close, it was becoming fashionable among young, upper-middle-class professionals, to spend what little vacation time Americans were allowed on ventures to the Dark Continent (emphasis on "dark"), and then to broadcast widely how transformative these experiences had been personally. Just a couple years before, yuppies were unapologetically booking their luxury hotels in Miami, Prague, perhaps Cancun or Acapulco (but not the virtue trips the Canadians were on). Now a group of more conscientious, and self-conscious, consumers were setting their sights on "enriching experiences," as these were promoted by an Africa tourism industry growing by leaps and bounds, rather than the "conventional sun and sea vacations."

Visiting Africa, in my old, white, male mind, meant standing in awe before ancient Egypt and its magnificent pyramids (imitated only later, and poorly, by Nubians); bowing before ethereal Islamic architecture of the great North African civilizations; succumbing to the onslaught of Marrakesh color; rocking the Kasbah ... Wasn't this

enrichment enough? Not for these new connois-
seurs who, just as they'd been refining their tastes
in group wine appreciation classes to show their
sophistication and keep up with their peers, were
learning to narrow in on specific regions, one in
particular. Africa, to these discriminating shoppers, meant not only sub-Saharan Africa, where
black people were most likely to be found, but refining their palates further, West Central Africa,
where most of the slaves were once harvested.
Their goal was not so much to bushwhack out an
expanding path to discovery, as to make a carefully
mapped return to the scene of a crime.

"I travel to see great civilizations, not mud
huts," I was glad, in retrospect, to have stopped
short of saying when my friend, knowing what a
philistine I could be, announced she planned to
visit, of all miserable places in the world, Senegal. I wasn't being entirely fair. One of the earliest
Club Meds was, in fact, built in Senegal in the early 1960s, among several similar experimental "so-
cialist" utopias around the world for whites disaf-
fected with the evils of capitalism and eager to go
primitive. Paying guests on quests for noble savagery were told their money was no good around

there, and instead were given strings of beads to buy cocktails and other survival basics. Later on, Club Meds took a different turn, becoming hedonistic hideouts for wealthy whites seeking, not to go native for social justice, but to enjoy the freedom of letting their hair down to find new ways of self-indulging. Attitudes toward vacationing had changed again thirty-some years later when my friends were suddenly asking if I wanted to join them on guilt trips to ground zero of the slave trade, less fun vacations, to my mind, than stodgy religious retreats full of fire and brimstone. All an unrepentant sinner like me could say was the same thing I said to bright-eyed youngsters flocking to recolonize Detroit, the hometown I'd left in the seventies, never to return: "*Why?*"

I was yet to understand the full, moral significance of these invitations to voyage. A trend called "dark tourism" had already been catching on for decades when my young friend announced her virtue trip. Before these aficionados of local skin color had come of age and tapped into their trust funds, fans with a taste for the macabre were chasing various strains of shock value promised by sites around the globe. Monty Python satirized this strange trend in their 1980s film *The Meaning of Life*. A charmingly unsophisticated couple of American seniors are shown perusing a Hawaiian dinner menu in an authentic medieval English dungeon, oblivious to the screams of victims hanging from the walls and being poked, stretched, flayed, and burned alive for their dining pleasure. Other favorite destinations within this grim travel genre were the site of the Chernobyl nuclear disaster, the Cambodian genocide museum in Phnom Penh, and various Holocaust landmarks. Added to the usual menu of horror shows, in recent years, was the transformative cleansing promised by pilgrimage packages to Senegal with daytrips to Gorée (emphasis on gore), an island off the coast, the sobering spot where countless captives of color were held before shipping out to their final destinations. These white guilt trips offered chances for reflection, self-examination, perhaps self-flagellation. Simple relaxation, wild abandon, thrills and chills—or cultural communion with the best of human achievements, a constant draw to an old, white man like me—were old hat to the young elite.

While I waited for Disney to recreate Gorée's

famous "House of Slaves" in its theme parks, just down from the Haunted Mansion ride, white guilt trips became too transformative for my stomach as overly earnest friends, many of them now former, went on quests for ancient black grievances across the United States. Stops included the highly politicized National Museum of African American History and Culture in Washington, D.C.; the Mississippi Civil Rights Museum with its "unflinching eye on Mississippi's most shameful history"; the National Memorial for Peace and Justice in Alabama (known more darkly as the "National Lynching Memorial") which drove home historical lynchings in the U.S. by county, then reached far to connect these crimes of the distant past against American blacks to present "racial violence" of all sorts around the world; and then, of course, the slave quarters in old plantations of the Deep South.

"Sounds like fun!" I said when they were still bothering to ask if I'd come along. "Bring the whole family!"

This new taste for melodrama, even among society's supposedly best and brightest, renewed my appetite for healthy historical perspective. I was tempted, at the risk of alienating a remaining friend who'd called to share her "socially cognizant" travel plans, to remind her that slavery was as old as humanity, and that slaves in Africa were for domestic consumption long before being exported. By the time a growing global market grasped the trade potential, black African kings had spent centuries enslaving their own people by the thousands to use as payments for debts. Before Europeans even got in on the action, Arabs got in on the ground floor, and just as the Portuguese would soon learn, harvesting black slaves meant relying on local blacks to hunt down and shackle the product. Any honest history of slavery in Africa without mention of black complicity, and not unimaginably, black training and advising of white traders, would be a very selective part of the story, indeed. Slavery in Africa, I might have added, was by no means a special black thing, as over a million white people were enslaved in North Africa between the 16th and 18th centuries.[1]

Not to rob my friend of the guilt feelings that seemed to give new meaning to her life, but her white ancestors came from Eastern Europe to the New World after slavery had been abandoned here. Not only did her sin inheritance not include anyone who'd owned or sold slaves, but her earlier relations were likely slaves themselves. "You know," I liked so say to "woke" friends I cared less to keep than her, "if the Jews had just whined all these centuries about slavery—except on certain high holy days—they'd still be building (as legend says they once were) pyramids!"

Down that road before, I knew what potent juice this new "movement" was selling and knew that neither my facts, nor my dark humor, could compete. The exhilarating rush of a repentance, veneration, and redemption narrative had a powerful grip on throngs of young people who were awakening from their sheltered, helicoptered childhoods to the shocking revelation that, yes, bad things happened in the world, and who were demanding to know, *tout de suite*: "Who let this happen?"

The commodification of white guilt, this bottling of bad blood, was on its way to becoming the predominant theme in a culture whose frame of reference, to a generation steeped in the minutiae of "multiculturalism," "diversity," and "inclusion" of everyone's "own truth," was shrinking to the scope of the latest viral Tweet. Once again, in the interest of a broader understanding, my old, white, male mind couldn't resist casting the net wider and learning from mistakes of the past. This mad rush to identify with a "marginalized" people, to tap into melodramatized history with visits to exotic, faraway places, coincided with a new trend budding right at our doorsteps. Back home in my over-gentrified Greenwich Village neighborhood, it was hard to ignore the recent explosion of artisan coffee breweries, sometimes two or three per block, quickly replacing more humble and practical things of the past like grocery stores, bakeries, laundromats, shoe repairs, and most sadly: bookstores. Like the pricey wine purveyors and boutique beer breweries springing up everywhere to serve a generation struggling to define itself, each of these artisan coffee shops drew its own local clique. Regulars came to waste time on cell phones, play on computers, chat about how good they were and how bad everyone else was, but most importantly: to forge brand-name identities with a custom black brew out of reach, like my neighborhood and much of New York had become, to most of humanity, black, white, or whatever.

Had a charming antiquarian bookstore on West Fourth not been displaced by yet another clique of likeminded, over-caffeinated yuppies, it might have still displayed, for their edification in an old shop window, a first edition of Tom Wolfe's scathing social critique called *Radical Chic*. Published in 1970, ancient history to the new radicals and off their radar, this was a witty account of a high-minded party hosted by residents of an elegant Park Avenue duplex penthouse to honor an unlikely group of guests: the Black Panthers. Standing awkwardly in a congregation of ultra-privileged gathered to court a rough bunch that probably would be avoided on the street, the black militant, anti-white, anti-assimilationist, anti-cop, anti-capitalist revolutionaries, Wolfe observes firsthand, grab asparagus tips and bleu-cheese-and-nut balls from silver trays held by maids in passing. Simply by their attendance, the white movie stars, composers, actors and assorted intelligentsia wear their anti-establishment, pro-black sympathies—and, I imagine, many Jew-fros—as badges of pride, if not deflective shields.

Once upon a time, in that very antiquarian

bookshop window now full of over-caffeinated progressives discussing how good they are and how bad everyone else is, sat *Radical Chic*, its cover slightly worn and edges discolored. The illustration showed a clearly Caucasian hand grasping an espresso cup containing a tiny black man who looked perturbed.

The latest crop of radical-chic consumers, like those radical-chic socialites of another era, weren't as oblivious as they looked. Their posing could not hide a natural-born survival instinct—what made them an elite in the first place—a nagging suspicion that despite their proud chest-pounding for supporting "social justice," one moment, their self-deprecating attempts at self-doubt, the next, and their constant finger-pointing at other whites for being "so white," at the end of the day they were just as lily-white as me. West Central Africa wasn't the best place in the world for them to blend in. How about surviving a night on West Fourth Street? The new radicals would write off my getting profiled and attacked as partial payment for centuries of oppression, but the flipside of so much moral certainty was fear, that same fear we all felt trying to get home safely each night. Brown-nosers could kiss all the black ass they wanted, but if black people really had been, and were still being treated as badly as everyone said, then not even a savior complex was sure to save "woke" whities when the revolution, their Judgment Day, came. Nothing of this world could balance the scales of justice, so they could keep their spare change, disastrous reforms, grandiose promises of reparations. The best they could hope for was to land on "the right"—not the white— "side of history."

Fear makes people say, and do, some crazy things. I suspected whites vacationing in Senegal believed their teary-eyed pilgrimages somehow brought them closer to slaves of old, to their somewhat less comfy Atlantic crossings, and so to their descendents back home. Absurd as it may sound, over the years and in various ways, many whites have even strived, while giving blacks greater "visibility," to take cover in darkness by becoming black themselves. Racial repackaging seems a travesty to a cynic like me, but short of blacking themselves up and joining minstrel shows, becoming black has seemed, to many white folks, worth a try. Not unlike another recent fad, "identifying" as a member of the opposite biological sex, mimicking another race has often meant falling back into some pretty cookie-cutter cultural stereotypes one hoped had been overcome.

Another book by a dead white man to deserve a place in an antiquarian shop window is Norman Mailer's *The White Negro*, a classic title from 1957 that won't register to a culture distracted by a cacophony of "marginalized voices," and too politically correct to even tolerate the book's title. Mailer was bored with what he called the numbing conformity of American liberal society. So he proposed an alternative sort of conformity. Members of the young, educated elite were urged to become "existentialist" hipsters by tapping into what Mailer considered the black man's naturally careless attitude and lack of direction, his jazzy sexuality, and perhaps most offensive to anyone daring enough to pick up this book today, his tendency toward violence. Acting more black, Mailer seemed to be saying, was the way for white people to be less bored with themselves. The cover of *The White Negro* featured the photographed face of a college-aged male with clearly Caucasian features, only in reverse black-and-white, a negative image of a white person: a white negro!

This emulation of black stereotypes persists to the present day. I still can't hide my embarrassment each time I see some overbred, condescending white Ivy Leaguer pretending to prostrate himself before a black guy who, sadly enough, doesn't look offended. Baseball cap on backwards, like any self-respecting homie, the elite white guy edits his language, and body language, in vaudevillian ways to meet what he imagines, quite rightly, to be many a black guy's expectations. Lowering himself to discuss something easy like basketball, he peppers his speech with yos, holmeses, dawgz, and Whah up?s. Added to the ghetto talk is a new toughness in his WASP-y swag. He changes his posture, leaning forward, arms swaying in wide, embracing movements, fingers pointing and thumbs up like a rapper keeping to the beat. The black guy he's courting, rather than burst out laughing, typically chimes in with talk of bitches, hos, booté, and various things phat. They smack hands together in agreement, and this meeting of minds closes with one final, hearty high five, or whatever the latest secret handshake.

Thinking you should communicate with

black people in a carefully contrived way is bad enough. In recent years, on streets across New York City, I've heard whites actually apologizing for being white. One night a young guy who lives around the corner from me was explaining to a black guy, in a sarcastic tone, that he used to be "a white male model." He wasn't bragging, but was confessing, disgustedly, for ever thinking white males should be models for anything.

"You keep on kissing that black ass," I still wish I would have said to my self-effacing neighbor. "Why don't you just bend over?" I might have asked, if only I wasn't afraid the white guy and the black guy would unite in racial harmony to kick this racist old white guy's ass.

Caucasians telling blacks what they want to hear, even aping unflattering elements selectively borrowed from the black repertoire, were part of a broader movement of white people who wanted somehow to blend in for self-preservation, and at the same time, stand out from the crowd of unwashed whites by acting more black. Who can forget, even if they try, the fad for low-rise, saggy pants that exposed a young man's underwear, front and back, in full public view everywhere he went? Wearing pants this way was not adopting some neutral style, but was making a clear fashion statement about racial politics. It started with young, black males imitating their favorite rappers and career criminals, then soon spread to white rappers like Eminem and Justin Bieber, and young, white males across the country who were suddenly wearing their baggy jeans "on ground." I shall never forget how wild the audience went that night at New York's Limelight club when Mark "Marky Mark" Wahlberg got up on stage and showed his tighty-whities to fans who were mainly white, upper-middle-class, and gay. Calvin Klein was quick in the 1990s to capitalize on this latest attempt at aping ghetto culture. He sold many pairs of partially exposed underwear in magazine ads and on billboards, evading any charges of "cultural appropriation" he would surely incur today. More recently in 2021, designer Balenciaga wasn't so lucky, and was assailed for "racial insensitivity" and "racism" for selling pants with boxer briefs actually sewn in above a lowered waistline.[2]

There was always something "problematic" built into the image of a white guy with his bloomers showing. A clear reference to gang and prison culture in recent years, the ultimate origins, in the humble opinion of this old white man with hindsight for history, go back further than a desire to look tough and threatening. Quite the opposite from commanding respect, knowing the more distant roots might make even black guys think twice about wearing saggy pants. Still worn, though less commonly today, dropped trow resurrect a classic vaudeville gag, a standard comedic mishap performed for years by white actors, in blackface, playing clowns who somehow always managed to be losing their breeches. The recent ghetto fashion could also be attributed to the "clown pants" worn by circus clowns whose suspenders did them no good. "A clown with his pants falling down, Or the dance that's a dream of romance, Or the scene where the villain is mean," are the opening lines to the timeless tune "That's Entertainment."

There's even a group of whites committed to preserving this vaudevillian tradition, all but the blackface part. The National Clown Pantsing Project, or NCPP—not to be confused with the NAACP (at the time of writing, still not politically-corrected to NAAPOC)—is "an artistic endeavor and a social movement. A small, dedicated group of some of the nation's most talented, progressive and committed performance artists."[3]

Not all blacks have been proud of this look, or happy to see it reinforced by whites whose futures aren't as fragile as those of young black males. "Some people might not want to see your underwear," said Barack Obama, off-put in 2008. "I'm one of them."[4] Others have been alarmed. Fred Davis, a civil rights pioneer who marched with Martin Luther King, and a successful businessman with an insurance agency in Memphis, risked being called an "Uncle Tom" for putting his foot down on saggy pants to try and win the minds of misguided, self-sabotaging black youth. Davis spent thousands of his own money to rent a billboard urging them: "Show your mind. Not your behind." Stage right on the billboard stood a young black man wearing a cap, a gown, and a smile while holding a diploma to his chest. Stage left, like a blackface vaudeville clown, was a rising-rapper type whose bright blue boxers threatened to steal the show. The message was clear enough: Education and hard work, not looking like a fool. "Pull up your pants!" Davis implored black youth in an interview. "We didn't fight for thuggish mentality. We fought to create an opportunity for the generations that came behind us."[5] Behind, indeed. While concerned parties were urging youths to show their minds and not their behinds, blacks were falling further behind each year in reading, writing, and arithmetic. Working against the efforts of blacks like Davis were the radical-chic whites who praised and imitated, as Norman Mailer once did, their existential hipness.

Towns across the country have actually outlawed, on grounds of obscenity, saggy pants, inviting charges of white fragility. But aren't clothes meaningful? It is a favorite trick of the radical chic to send mixed signals, to say, in one breath, that imitating bad role models is harmless fun and clothes are neutral, and then to turn around and say that ghetto fashions are vested with cultural significance and white people who wear them are in fact guilty of "appropriation." Trayvon Martin gets shot wearing a hoodie, and suddenly clothes are a mere pretense for "profiling." Reams have been published on the meanings of clothes. Choosing to buy an article with a specific label, cut and colored in a particular style from distinctive materials to connote wealth, social standing, taste, political sympathies, other allegiances—but also saying that the projected meanings of clothing should not be interpreted—is trying to have it both ways. The people who shoot young black males because of what they're wearing are mainly other black males who belong to gangs. Certainly, not all blacks who wear hoodies are criminals, but finding a description of a crime suspect that does not include mention of a "hooded sweatshirt" can be difficult. Similarly, not every young black male to wear saggy pants will end up in prison, or be shot by another black male in saggy pants. But the chances are quite good. The least white people could do for blacks would be to stop reinforcing the wrong role models.

So many white people are so bent on being black that it's hard not to make fun of them. A journal of satire called *The Babylon Bee* recently published then posted on social media a helpful guide to self-darkening, "7 Ways You Can Be Less White." Suggestions included "Rip off all your skin," "Take dance classes," and "Throw out all your ranch dressing."[6] As usual, I got myself into hot water for making an off-color comment. "The best way to be less white and more black," I wrote, "would be to start shooting black people."

The "community standards" police did not appreciate my dark sense of humor. My comment was instantly deleted and I spent another three days in Facebook jail.

ENDNOTES

1 Jeff Grabmeier, "When Europeans Were Slaves: Research Suggests White Slavery Was Much More Common Than Previously Believed," *Ohio State News*, March 7, 2004, https://news.osu.edu/when-europeans-were-slaves--research-suggests-white-slavery-was-much-more-common-than-previously-believed/

2 Sophie Miller, "Balenciaga's $1,200 sagging pants are being decried as racist," *Fortune*, September 7, 2021, https://fortune.com/2021/09/07/balenciaga-1200-sagging-pants-decried-as-racist-online/.

3 The National clown pantsing project (sic), Facebook page, January 20, 2023.

4 Ben Smith, "Barack Obama does not want to see your underwear," Politico, November 3, 2008, https://www.politico.com/blogs/ben-smith/2008/11/barack-obama-does-not-want-to-see-your-underwear-013848.

5 Jay Dillon, "Former civil rights activist says 'pull up your pants' in billboard," Fox 25, September 17, 2013, https://okcfox.com/archive/former-civil-rights-activist-says-pull-up-your-pants-in-billboard.

6 "7 Ways You Can Be Less White," *The Babylon Bee*, February 22, 2021, https://babylonbee.com/news/7-ways-you-can-be-less-white.

three

BLACK PEOPLE
BEING WHITE

During my many years of dodging offended black people who approach me from behind, or threaten face-to-face to kick my white old ass or do damage worse than that, I've kept tending to routine matters of health maintenance—in case I manage to survive these daily ordeals with people still angry at me over slavery.

One of these routine health matters has been the occasional colonoscopy. So far, I've had only one. The day of that procedure, I was naturally a bit nervous, as anyone might be their first time regardless of race, gender, color or creed. In fact the colonoscopy, a necessary and very common way to try and ward off death, might be called the new Great Leveler. It carries no social status, and is even embarrassing to talk about. It does not require affirmative action, and spares no one. I sat nervously in the hospital waiting area with a diverse array of patients wearing, like me, flimsy gowns and stripped of all proof of "identity" but wristbands. Together, we felt weak and queasy after a day of gruesome prep work but were hoping for the best. Finally, my name was called. I rose slowly, in case of dizziness, braced myself, and headed down the hall to be wheeled to the procedure room and anesthetized.

I'd been down a similar path a couple years prior, and with the same doctor who'd performed an endoscopy and happily found nothing to worry about. An extraordinarily kind man, patient with patients and sensitive to their concerns, a caring doctor who'd made the effort to talk me through the last procedure, he was a paragon of bedside manner and made me feel in good hands. He also just happened to be white. While I was wheeled down the hall to be knocked senseless, I heard the voice of another of his patients, one who was seated alongside me in the waiting room when my name was called. He sounded upset, and his shouting added stress to what was already a stressful situation for everyone.

"Always making the black man wait!" he cried from somewhere down the hall. "Black people are always last!" he kept repeating, again and again, at the top of his voice.

While the angry black man wailed, in grand oratorical style like a Baptist preacher testifying to an act of injustice, I wondered why my doctor would have chosen to single out someone, to make any one of us, due to skin color, wait longer to be anally probed. It occurred to me, without much forethought, that he hadn't, though our dear doctor had reason to be concerned about this black man seeking greater "visibility." In a growing climate of victimhood and fear, of knowing "your own truth," of jumping to conclusions about police shootings of black males and being told to always "believe women"—however unbelievable the woman—my doctor surely wanted to avoid allegations of racism, no matter how flimsy, that might have been believed simply because the right person had made them.

Yes, our doctor was white, but I don't believe he cared about the color of an ass he was treating. The outraged black man was just making trouble because he didn't want to wait his turn and he was probably used to getting his way. Approaching the room of the dreaded procedure, I would've gladly given up my place in line, if only to spare our nice doctor some grief as the black man's manufactured grievances still echoed down the hall. Flat on my back, passing one of the side rooms, I saw the doctor standing in the doorway and raised a hand to say hello, but realized he was hiding to avoid an incident when he held a finger to his mouth to say: "Shhhhh." Before I went under, as I slipped toward not caring, I remember wishing someone would shoot up and shut up the jackass down the hall.

One thing to remember if you're visiting black culture, or dealing with a black person visiting your own: Some black people do not like to be kept waiting. They also don't like to receive service they feel isn't worthy of them. Returning to this question of race in restaurants, it is an endless source of wonderment to me that white employees, having undergone mandatory training in how "unconsciously biased" they are against black people, having been told how "privileged" they are to be working these grueling jobs alongside them, still manage somehow to offend black co-workers, and black customers, with their lack of a new thing called "racial literacy" by the diversity-and-inclusion officers. Despite so much drilling and shaming, white people working in a variety of industries apparently still don't know how to treat black people, whose culture seems so foreign and removed, and whose very high attrition rates from the workplace blacks attribute to not feeling they "belong" or are "safe."[1] The only thing that fills me with more wonder than how insensitive whites remain to "the black experience" is how certain blacks manage to devote so much time and energy on a constant vigil against anything offensive—only to find other blacks more offensive to them than the whites are!

The history of black people's difficulty in not offending each other is long and troubling. Over the past couple years alone, and looking only at restaurant incidents, there have been a great many senseless and brutal acts of black-on-black violence, and over matters that seem trivial to a culturally insensitive old white guy like me. The latest hypersensitive stand, at the time of writing, taken on a matter of black honor was the fatal shooting of a young black male working at a McDonald's in Brooklyn—by a young black male customer over French fries his mamma said were too cold.[2] You can't make this stuff up.

And I don't have to. Another recent case of much ado about nothing, made by the usual suspect who dindu nuffin, was at a McDonald's in Midtown Manhattan where it seems a black barista put too much sugar in a black customer's coffee for his taste. Forget about putting cream in da coffay. The oversweetened black offendant argued with a black security guard and then stabbed someone else. That'll make them think twice before adding that second teaspoon.[3] No one, not even another "person of color," is spared in breaches of black decorum. A few blocks uptown in Harlem, a young Hispanic man working as a cashier at McDonald's was stabbed multiple times with a box cutter and left in a coma by an aggrieved black male customer. The reason remains unclear.[4] This is to list but a few of the countless examples of how certain New Yorkers settle disputes over the finer points of restaurant etiquette.

Shootings, stabbings, beatings—restaurant employees across the country, black, white, Hispanic or whatever, are currently at a loss on how to better please this demanding bunch of patrons. Again quite recently, a black woman shot four employees at an Oklahoma McDonald's simply for not letting her sit in a area closed due to Covid restrictions![5] Two fifteen-year-old black males pulled up to a McDonald's drive-thru window in Springfield, Massachusetts, and shot an employee ten times with a BB gun for no reason at all.[6] I imagine if they'd had some beef, they would have used real guns. A twenty-seven-year-old black male customer was told by a sixteen-year-old black male worker at a Wendy's in Phoenix he would have to pay extra to enjoy an additional dipping sauce with his chicken nuggets—so the customer shot the boy in the head and left him disabled.[7] A saucy black woman in another Phoenix Wendy's was upset over getting fries not as hot as, and nuggets even spicier than, her temper. She threw both orders back at the worker and is wanted for assault.[8] Twin sisters named Bryanna Johnson and

Breanta Johnson (I'm not making this up) ordered some burgers in a Milwaukee restaurant (a short drive from where a black supremacist had recently run over 62 people during a Christmas parade), but after making trouble from the moment they sat down, they said the service was bad and they weren't going to pay. So their food was taken away. Bryanna shot the young Hispanic waiter, father of a two-year-old boy, in the face, causing him to fall, then Breanta stomped on his face.[9] What's the best way to resolve a work-related dispute? Shoot the other black male employee, as just happened in a St. Louis McDonald's.[10] Shoot your manager, as another black male just did in Atlanta.[11] "Kill My Landlord," Eddy Murphy's classic sketch for *Saturday Night Live*, needs to be updated to include restaurant grievances.

Meanwhile, back in the Big Apple, a Filipino male immigrant was recently minding his own business at a McDonald's across the street from Madison Square Garden, a restaurant I've been to many times. A few months prior, out front, a black man had recently tried to rob me as I lay bleeding in the middle of Seventh Avenue after a serious bike accident. This time, an entirely different black man (I mention so as not to be accused of profiling) entered the McDonald's and savagely beat the Asian man (on camera, as most of these black-on-Asian attacks), leaving his victim in critical condition.[12] Uptown, another Asian person, a young, slightly-built hostess at a famous Italian restaurant called Carmine's (very popular among blacks), was repeatedly punched by three of the grotesquely obese walruses described in Chapter 1. (Not the same walruses! Different walruses!). They were offended because the hostess had asked for proof of Covid vaccination, as every restaurant in the city was required by law to do at the time. Black Lives Matter sprang into action and protested in front of Carmine's.[13] Friends and I had dinner there to show our support against Black Lives Matter.

Last but not least—and not last by a long shot—is a troubling tragedy that will stay in the hearts and minds of many of us New Yorkers for years to come. A Puerto Rican woman, age 19, was recently working the night shift at a Burger King in Harlem to save money for nursing school, when a young black man entered wearing a mask and holding a gun. He pistol-whipped a male customer and punched the female manager, then placed his order with the young woman at the counter. She was able to hand him $100 but was still struggling to open the register when he shot her dead.[14] I guess the service wasn't snappy enough.

The young woman's family and community joined to protest her senseless death and mourn their loss. They demanded her cold-blooded, hotheaded killer be found and brought to justice. Police were able to track him down. It turned out he'd been an employee at the Burger King, and had seven prior arrests in New York City. "Why am I guilty?" he asked the police as they took him away in handcuffs. "*You know they charge n____s every day?*" he asked a crowd witnessing the trickle-down effects of academic race theory on someone who'd never been to college. "*Where's our reparations for four hundred fucking years of slavery?*" he asked, showing that although he'd likely never read *The New York Times*, his work was indirectly influenced by the so-called "1619 Project" that sought to make slavery the basis of black identity, the get-out-of-jail-free card in "progressive" justice reform, a reason for reparations, the founding principle of the United States, the cause of obesity in walruses—and now slavery was his excuse for murdering a young Hispanic woman who wanted to be a nurse. "America is gonna BURN!" he cried as they put him in the squad car.[15]

Could the black crime problem be due to something as simple as believing the wrong narratives or choosing the wrong role models? "Professors think things were better when women and minorities just acted more like white guys," read the headline to an opinion piece by a white male lawyer attacking a white Ivy League law professor and her white male colleague for presumptuously pointing out, in *The Philadelphia Inquirer*, some bad values and behavior problems in certain populations.[16] Already by 2017, any constructive advice from white people to help anyone else improve their lives was equated with expecting everyone to act "white," unless the purveyors of free advice were radical-chic white people always ready to run to the defense of blacks, any blacks, so long as they were acting sufficiently "black." Who better than they to castigate these advocates of "white superiority"?

Professors Amy Wax and Larry Alexander had the poor taste to tell an increasingly "woke" world, in case it hadn't already noticed, about the self-destructive course some Americans, including many black people, had been on since the 1960s, and to suggest what might be encouraged to get them back on track before yet another generation was lost. "Homicidal violence plagues inner cities," was one of their offensive claims. If this had not been a short opinion piece, they might have gone into detail by mentioning that blacks had long been committing a wildly disproportionate number of violent crimes in the U.S., and mainly against other blacks. But these were facts, no matter how provable, one simply didn't mention in polite society. "Almost half of all children are born out of wedlock" was another racial faux pas, even though the trend had been most disastrous to black people whose illegitimacy rate surpassed 70%, by far the highest of any group in the country, and with clear correlations in vastly higher crime and incarceration rates. "Many college students lack basic skills" was an inconvenient truth based, not only on testing and dropout rates, but on Wax's own experience teaching at an Ivy League law school. While white people were being educated in "racial literacy," real literacy, said by the left to be culturally biased, left much to be desired. "I don't think I've ever seen a black student graduate in the top quarter of the class, and rarely, rarely, in the top half," she later told one of my favorite intellectuals (who just happens to be black), Professor Glenn Loury (who has recently contributed to a GoFundMe campaign to save her job), in a podcast on affirmative action. Like so many self-made people from the working class, Wax had no patience for preferential treatment or for victimhood narratives.

Wax & Co. continued dusting off daily facts of life the radical-chic had been trying to sweep under a rug for the prior half-century. "The single-parent, antisocial habits prevalent among some working-class whites" and "the anti 'acting white' rap culture of inner-city blacks," they wrote, were "not suited for a First World, 21st-century environment." More simple truisms, but not suited for polite company. What arrogant advice did the two white supremacists offer against this plight they witnessed in a culture once so vibrant and full of hope but now on a crash course?

"Get married before you have children," they suggested, oh-so politely, what I would have volunteered with no pretense to delicacy: Stop spraying the streets with tomorrow's criminals that don't stand a chance! "Get the education you need for gainful employment, work hard, and avoid idleness. Go that extra mile for your employer or client. Be a patriot, ready to serve the country. Be neighborly, and charitable. Avoid coarse language in public. Be respectful of authority. Eschew substance abuse and crime."

In other words: Do what the rest of us— white, black, or whatever—must do, not only to thrive, but to survive in this particular culture at this point in time. Not once did Wax & Co. recommend looking up to the famous thug rappers, role models to so many black youths, still shooting each other after becoming multi-millionaires, thereby weakening the "poverty" defense for rampant black-on-black crime. Nor did they flirt with black separatism, as so many of their radical-chic colleagues, safe in cushy, tenured university jobs, encouraged average black folks to do. I don't presume to speak for America's black middle class, but I can guess they found nothing offensive about two white people promoting the very values that had been the secret to their own success, or objectionable about this honest advice to shun the supposedly "black" culture they spent their lives escaping. "Everyone wants to go to countries ruled by white Europeans." True enough, but another truism banned from politically correct circles. The rest of the world, including those black African immigrants resistant to the ramblings of radical-chic revolutionaries, doesn't dream of being American because they resent the values and habits that have made America such a desirable place to be in the first place. Only a certain subset of homegrown blacks, prey to the wrong advisors, want to escape this perceived prison to which they've been consigned since slavery.

Here's where Wax & Co. got into some real trouble with polite society: "All cultures are not equal. Or at least they are not equal in preparing people to be productive in an advanced economy."[17] This is something that can no longer be suggested, much less said, at our present culmination of 60s cultural relativism. The myth of value-free judgment is no longer believed to be a myth, but rather has been made into an imperative article of faith. It's the same crooked path taken by "progressives" who claim to care about wom-

en's rights, in one breath, but then defend mandatory coverings on women because, well, these are
different cultures that may not care about wom-
en's rights, but we need to respect their customs
or we're no better than colonialists.

I've often wondered why the radical-chic elite
would want to defend the worst possible behaviors they would warn their own children against,
to encourage the dark cynicism of this new strain
of "black culture," to sabotage the lives of those
who (let's be honest) might not know better, to
dissuade blacks from doing what they themselves
(or the sources of their trust funds) have done
to be successful—if not to hold back black people by keeping them from having what *they* have.
Because this would make them "white," and we
wouldn't want that.

Ivory-tower theorizing, based largely on the
writings of a dead white man named Karl Marx,
but now boiled down to simplistic assumptions
about skin color and personality instead of class,
and facile "intersectionality" grids fast replacing
true critical thought in universities, has all had
far-reaching effects. The dubious motives of the
academics have in fact been institutionalized at the

highest levels, and in ways that should make Amy Wax's suggestions on self-improvement seem like wholesome parental concerns. The National Museum of African American History and Culture in Washington, D.C., saw fit to publish, two months after George Floyd's death in 2020, a "whiteness" chart listing those behaviors, qualities, and values it said were essential to "white people and their traditions," but that anyone darker had a duty to resist. Among the list of loathsome things said to be essential to "whiteness" were: "decision-making" "must always 'do something' about a situation," "emphasis on scientific method: objective, rational linear thinking; cause and effect relationships; quantitative emphasis," "plan for future," "delayed gratification," "follow rigid time schedules," "hard work is the key to success," "individuals assumed to be in control of their environment: *'You get what you deserve.'*"[18]

Anyone who has ever known a lazy, spendthrift Caucasian rich kid in a Gender Studies program, or a raving, irrational, lesbian-feminista social justice warrior with white skin, lavender hair, and a victim complex, might take issue with some items on this list. Spoiled, mindless whites, if ever they took time off activism to think, should be offended by being labeled with certain "white" values to which they don't subscribe. Not since the outlandish race inventories compiled by eugenic theorists in the 19th and 20th centuries, has there been such a brazen act of overgeneralization about cultural differences, or a more simplistic attempt to reduce these differences essentially to race. The clear tendencies Amy Wax pointed to in certain communities were cast in a new shade. Black Americans were told, in so many words, not only that "white culture" was foreign to their own native instincts, but that they should not even attempt to assimilate because they *could not*. Instead, it was the duty of non-whites to stop being prisoners of the "white dominant culture" and to look elsewhere for their role models. I'll leave it to proud, hardworking members of the black working class, and proud, hardworking members of the black middle class, including African immigrants who fare far better on average than homegrown blacks—not because they were spared anything "systemic" or "structural" the native homies are said to endure, but because they refuse to be poisoned by radical-chic defeatism—to share their

feelings with a federally-funded Smithsonian In-
stitution museum located on the National Mall.

The real crimes against black people weren't
included on the Smithsonian's list. The first of
these crimes was: Overestimating causes such as
"poverty" for self-destructive violence on a mass
scale. (While black poverty rates are comparable
nationwide to those of Hispanics, black violent
crime rates are disproportionately higher; and the
black poverty rate in New York City is actually
lower than that of Hispanics who do not slaugh-
ter each other, or spray the streets with wild, fa-
therless kids, even remotely like blacks do).[19] The
second crime: Encouraging self-destructive attitudes that set black people back generations. The
third crime: Lowering standards, based on talent
and merit, in education and in the workplace, to
accommodate the underqualified because of their
skin color. The fourth crime: Concocting pseudo-
scientific psychobabble like "Post-Traumatic Slave
Syndrome" (and validating this non-condition
with capital letters as "PTSS").[20]

The real racism, and what's most offensive
to Professor John McWhorter (another of my favorite intellectuals who just happen to be black),

is this widespread defense of black exceptional-
ism based on the unspoken assumption that black
Americans are inferior, or at least different, and
shouldn't be subjected to the same criteria as successful whites, Asians, Hispanics, or even other
blacks—because, well, slavery.

"An enlightened America is supposed to hold
a public figure accountable for her ideas," wrote
McWhorter, in his book *Woke Racism*, about one
of the left's favorite token blacks, Nikole Hannah-Jones.[21] The *New York Times* journalist and
"Genius Grant" recipient had won a Pulitzer Prize
for doing some pretty shabby scholarship in her
so-called "1619 Project." That shabbiness was
called out by historians across the political spec-
trum, and intellectuals across the races, and her
claim that colonists had fought the Revolutionary
War to preserve slavery became, to borrow that favorite term of today's new left, problematic. The
true founding date of the country, Hannah-Jones
had us believing for a moment, was not 1776, as
traditionally accepted, but 1619, the date the first
slaves arrived. The very thesis of her project, and
its title, the very Pulitzer that Hannah-Jones was
awarded, rested on the claim that because the Rev-

olutionary War was fought to keep slavery—which it wasn't—the founding of the United States, its core values, beliefs, and institutions, not only were tainted by slavery, but were defined by it.

"Woke" white folks had to be immensely relieved. It seemed, for one brief but righteous moment, they would not need to wait for the end-time and the final Judgment Day to land "on the right side of history." They could have their re-demption right here and now, online and in real time.

Dashed dreams of instant karma aside, this was also to be a new record in the fight for black "visibility," and despite the glaring error, "cultural etiquette," as McWhorter called it, dictated damage control.[22] The *New York Times*, once considered the newspaper of record, quietly edited erroneous passages from its online edition. The Pulitzer people quietly ignored the matter and did not rescind the award. Public apologies, in any event, would not have mattered. The print edition of The *NYT Magazine* had already landed on doorsteps around the world. The cover featured a photograph of what might have been the Atlantic Ocean. Superimposed over waves that had presumably once carried slave ships was a paragraph announcing "The 1619 Project" and unveiling its thesis: "America was not yet America, but this was the moment it began. No aspect of the country that would be formed here has been untouched by the 250 years of slavery that followed."[23] The Pulitzer Center had already released a children's school curriculum based on a project with a flawed thesis already gone viral. The notion dropped over the Atlantic Ocean had already slipped into the water supply: America was now officially all about slavery and the ongoing struggle of black people. At least in the minds of those who wanted to see it that way, like the black man who murdered the young Puerto Rican woman and blamed his arrest on slavery.

John McWhorter was right to be offended by condescending wokies giving Hannah-Jones a pass. Unafraid to call a spade a spade, he wrote: "White people patting her on the head for being 'brave' or 'getting her views out there,' rather than regretting that she slipped up and wishing her better luck next time, are bigots of a kind."[24] I would add that members of polite society did not want to criticize "a black woman speaking her mind," as someone claiming to be Hannah-Jones once described herself to me in an email, because the stakes were too high. The eternal salvation of wokies aside, any admission of rigging selections would have to include black complicity in this lowering of standards—or did they guess black people were too blinded by "identity" to see they were being played?

Efforts to package and commodify blackness—this time, targeting black consumers—have led to curious conclusions. Anyone with a good grasp of history knows there is nothing basically black about slavery, and not all blacks define themselves by slavery, by what followed, or by what they are no longer: African. Attempts to return to some imagined pure and unspoiled state prior to lamented events can lead to disappointment. I myself became aware of the dangers of romanticizing the past when it one day occurred to me that most of my Great Aunt Mary's recipes from "the old country" of Lithuania—somehow involved Bisquick. Despite the rapid growth in an industry devoted to helping people find themselves with pop genealogy, DNA, and Ancestry.com, after many recent "heritage trips" taken by black

Americans to West Africa, these "life-changing" pilgrimages have convinced only a few thousand tourists to stay. "Despite some initial setbacks," says United Nations Africa Renewal, "people of African descent continue to migrate to the continent, though not in the expected droves."[25] For most black Americans seeking to live in the past, it's been a round-trip passage back to the dreaded U.S. and all its whiteness.

If slavery and tenuous ties to Africa aren't enough to make black Americans special, then what is it, other than the violence and some very good black music, that sets black Americans apart from everyone else in this "white dominant culture"?

Not even the bad behavior of an aggrieved subset of black Americans is distinctively "black," according to Jason Riley (another of my favorite intellectuals who just happen to be black). "A sad irony of the black cultural obsession with avoiding white behavior," as Riley wrote in his book *Please Stop Helping Us: How Liberals Make It Harder for Blacks to Succeed*, "is that the habits and attitudes associated with ghetto life today can be traced not to Mother Africa but to Europeans who immigrated to the American South," starting in the late 18th century.[26] Referring to books by Thomas Sowell (another of my favorites who happen to be black), *Black Rednecks and White Liberals*, and Grady McWhiney, author of *Cracker Culture*, Riley points out some uncanny similarities between the culture brought over by certain rough, loud, lawbreaking Irish, Scottish, and Welsh—and black ghetto culture today: "an aversion to work, proneness to violence, neglect of education, sexual promiscuity, improvidence, drunkenness, lack of entrepreneurship, reckless searches for excitement, lively music and dance, and a style of religious oratory marked by strident rhetoric, unbridled emotions, and flamboyant imagery."[27]

It is, I would add, difficult to imagine gospel music or blues without the influence of Scottish hymns, or most of the "black" music that followed, without a little thing called tonality, an invention of Western white males. Setting aside the annoying, cloying, overacted, Baptist-preacher ravings of black intellectuals like Michael Eric Dyson and Cornel West—and the loudmouth, snake-oil-peddling crackers like "whiteness studies" expert Robin DiAngelo—what matters most is how destructive certain other aspects of "black" culture continue to be to black Americans.

"Most whites have of course abandoned this behavior, and have risen socioeconomically as a result," wrote Riley. "How ironic that so many blacks cling to these practices in an effort to avoid 'acting white.' And how tragic that so many liberals choose to put an intellectual gloss on black cultural traits that deserve disdain. The civil rights movement, properly understood, was about equal opportunity. But a group must be culturally equipped to seize it. Blacks today on balance remain ill equipped, and the problem isn't white people."[28]

Ironic, indeed. If black intellectuals acting white are right, then this violence-prone, literacy-resistant subset of black Americans isn't acting black at all, but has been acting like white guys all along—just not the *right* white guys.

ENDNOTES

1 Like the very high college dropout rates among blacks, very high black attrition rates in the workplace are concerning. Companies hire people based on their skin color, but they have a hard time keeping them. Blacks are over 30% more likely than whites to plan leaving a new job within the first two years. Even Google, whose very product might be said to be wokeness, is having a terrible time sustaining "diversity." Melanie Hanson, "College Graduation Statistics: College Dropout Rate Demographics," *Education Data Initiative*, June 12, 2022, https://educationdata.org/college-dropout-rates; Erica Pandey, "Corporate America's revolving door for black employees," Axios, November 17, 2020, https://www.axios.com/2020/11/17/corporate-america-black-employee-turnover-rate; Steven Musil, "Google diversity report shows increased attrition rate for black women," CNET, July 1, 2021, https://www.cnet.com/tech/tech-industry/google-diversity-report-shows-increased-attrition-rate-for-black-women/.

2 Lee Brown, "McDonald's worker shot over cold fries has died," *New York Post*, August 5, 2022, https://nypost.com/2022/08/05/brooklyn-mcdonalds-worker-shot-over-cold-fries-has-died/.

3 Amanda Woods, "NYC man stabbed over Mc-

Donald's coffee dispute," *New York Post*, September 22, 2021, https://nypost.com/2021/09/22/nyc-man-stabbed-over-mcdonalds-coffee-dispute/.

4 Erica Byfield and Romney Smith, "Cops ID Man Who Allegedly Put NYC McDonald's Worker in Coma After Box Cutter Attack," NBC New York, March 12, 2022, https://www.nbcnewyork.com/news/local/cops-id-man-who-put-nyc-mcdonalds-worker-in-coma-after-box-cutter-attack-ny-only/3595897/.

5 Ken Miller, "Gloricia Woody shoots Mc-Donald's workers over closing dining area," *The Washington Times*, May 7, 2020, https://www.washingtontimes.com/news/2020/may/7/gloricia-woody-shoots-mcdonalds-workers-over-closi/.

6 Lexi Oliver, Josh Daley, and Ryan Trowbridge, "Police: McDonald's employee shot with BB gun at drive-thru," Western Mass News, August 9, 2022, https://www.westernmassnews.com/2022/08/09/police-mcdonalds-employee-shot-with-bb-gun-drive-thru/.

7 Jessive Schladebeck, "Teen employed at Phoenix Wendy's shot in the head in dispute over barbecue sauce," *New York Daily News*, January 15, 2022, https://www.nydailynews.com/news/crime/ny-wendys-shooting-teen-suspect-arrested-20220115-n2jvc7us2nbxfohl2om5xcyudu-story.html.

8 Louis Casiano, "Unhappy Wendy's customer

assaults employee over unspicy nuggets: cops,"
New York Post, June 21, 2022, https://nypost.
com/2022/06/21/unhappy-wendys-customer-as-
saults-employee-over-unspicy-nuggets-cops/.

9 Courtney Sisk, "Newly released video shows
customer shoot George Webb employee in face,"
WISN 12, May 20, 2022, https://www.wisn.com/
article/newly-released-video-shows-customer-
shoot-george-webb-employee-in-face/40064152.

10 Sam Clancy and Pepper Baker, "Man charged
with murder in deadly shooting of McDonald's
co-worker," 5 On Your Side, June 7, 2022, https://
www.ksdk.com/article/news/crime/man-shot-to-
death-outside-mcdonalds-st-louis/63-985fc6e4-
34dd-4e53-b230-70803310ac9b.

11 Miles Montgomery, "Employee who shot Mc-
Donald's manager arrested, officials say," Atlanta
News First, June 10, 2022, https://www.atlantan-
ewsfirst.com/2022/06/10/dekalb-county-jail-of-
ficial-employee-who-shot-mcdonalds-manager-ar-
rested/.

12 Carl Samson, "Repeat offender not charged with
assault after beating Asian victim in NYC robbery,"
NextShark, April 1, 2022, https://nextshark.com/
repeat-offender-not-charged-assault.

13 Lee Brown, "Carmine's releases new footage of
attack on staff amid BLM protests targeting eat-
ery," *New York Post*, September 21, 2021, https://
nypost.com/2021/09/21/nyc-eatery-carmines-re-

leases-new-surveillance-video-of-attack/.

14 Tina Moore, Kevin Sheehan, and Jorge Fitz-Gibbon, "Teen gunned down while working her shift at NYC Burger King, cops say," *New York Post*, January 9, 2022, https://nypost.com/2022/01/09/teen-gunned-down-while-working-shift-at-nyc-burger-king-cops/.

15 Ben Feuerherd, "Burger King murder suspect yells 'f—k you all' at angry crowd as he's led out of station," *New York Post*, January 14, 2022, https://nypost.com/2022/01/14/east-harlem-residents-shout-at-burger-king-murder-suspect/.

16 Joe Patrice, "Law Professors Say White '50s Culture Is Superior, Other Racist Stuff," Above The Law, August 11, 2017, https://abovethelaw.com/2017/08/law-professors-say-white-50s-culture-is-superior-other-racist-stuff/.

17 Amy Wax and Larry Alexander, "Paying the price for breakdown of the country's bourgeois culture," *The Philadelphia Inquirer*, August 9, 2017, https://www.inquirer.com/philly/opinion/commentary/paying-the-price-for-breakdown-of-the-countrys-bourgeois-culture-20170809.html; GianCarlo Canaparo and Abby Kassal, "Who Suffers the Most From Crime Wave?" The Heritage Foundation, April 12, 2022, https://www.heritage.org/crime-and-justice/commentary/who-suffers-the-most-crime-wave; "The downside to social uplift," The Glenn Show, September 11, 2017, https://

www.youtube.com/watch?v=cb9Ey-SsNsg

18 Sam Dorman, "DC museum criticized for saying 'delayed gratification' and 'decision-making' are aspects of 'whiteness,'" Fox News, July 15, 2020, https://www.foxnews.com/us/dc-museum-graphic-whiteness-race.

19 "Poverty rate in the United States by ethnicity group 2021," *Statista*, September 30, 2022, https://www.statista.com/statistics/200476/us-poverty-rate-by-ethnic-group/; Allen J. Beck, Race and Ethnicity of Violent Crime Offenders and Arrestees, 2018, U.S. Department of Justice, *Statistical Brief*, January 2021, https://bjs.ojp.gov/content/pub/pdf/revcoa18.pdf; "Expanded Homicide Data Table 6 / Murder: Race, Sex, and Ethnicity of Victim by Race, Sex, and Ethnicity of Offender, 2019," Uniform Crime Reports, https://ucr.fbi.gov/crime-in-the-u.s/2019/crime-in-the-u.s.-2019/tables/expanded-homicide-data-table-6.xls; Matt Clarke, "U.S. DOJ Statistics on Race and Ethnicity of Violent Crime Perpetrators," Prison Legal News, June 1, 2021, https://www.prisonlegalnews.org/news/2021/jun/1/us-doj-statistics-race-and-ethnicity-violent-crime-perpetrators/; "Latinos continue to have the highest poverty rates of all race and ethnic groups in New York City," Center for Latin American, Caribbean and Latino Studies (CLACLS) at The Graduate Center of The City University of New York, November 28, 2022, https://clacls.gc.cuny.edu/2022/11/28/latinos-

continue-to-have-the-highest-poverty-rates-of-all-race-and-ethnic-groups-in-new-york-city/; Crime and Enforcement Activity in New York City (Jan 1 – Dec 31, 2021): "Murder and Non-Negligent Manslaughter Victim, Suspect, Arrestee Race/Ethnicity," https://www.nyc.gov/assets/nypd/downloads/pdf/analysis_and_planning/year-end-2021-enforcement-report.pdf; Roger Clegg, "Percentage of Births to Unmarried Women," *National Review*, February 10, 2020, https://www.nationalreview.com/corner/percentage-of-births-to-unmarried-women/.

20 Joy DeGruy, *Post-Traumatic Slave Syndrome: America's Legacy of Enduring Injury and Healing* (Joy DeGruy Publications, Inc., 2017).

21 John McWhorter, *Woke Racism: How a New Religion Has Betrayed Black America* (Portfolio/Penguin), 2021, 108.

22 Ibid., 108.

23 "The 1619 Project," *The New York Times Magazine*, August 18, 2019, https://www.nytimes.com/interactive/2019/08/14/magazine/1619-america-slavery.html.

24 McWhorter, *Woke Racism*, 109.

25 Efam Dovi, "African-Americans resettle in Africa," Africa Renewal, April, 2015, https://www.un.org/africarenewal/magazine/april-2015/african-americans-resettle-africa.

26 Jason Riley, *Please Stop Helping Us: How Liber-*

als Make It Harder for Blacks to Succeed (Encounter Books, 2014), 56-57.

27 Ibid., 57.

28 Ibid., 57-58.

four

SAINT GEORGE

The first images in the news I found striking enough to note in the early days of the Covid pandemic were those of black people committing violent crimes.

These in themselves were nothing to write home about. I was born in Detroit, still murder capital of the world in the early 80s when I arrived in New York, a close second for that dubious honor. "Black crime," a redundant expression, as far as I was concerned, came as no surprise in my new home where I was mugged twice in my first year before becoming more streetwise. Forty years later, the usual acts committed by the usual "suspects" were still standard fare.

One thing was different in the strange new world of Covid: Black criminals were often wearing masks. Caught on camera delivering the usual sucker punches to elderly people on the sidewalk, savagely beating gays and Asians they happened upon, attacking Jewish children on their way to school, shooting up workers and customers in fast-food restaurants, harassing, stabbing and pushing subway riders onto tracks—slaughtering each other—were blacks behind masks, like white villains in old Western movies. Victims of masked black violence and Covid fatalities seemed two sides of the same coin. Their numbers grew simultaneously and exponentially.

I used to say black criminals were too dumb to know there were cameras almost everywhere in this day and age, that getting away with even the most random violent crime, even if they managed to get away, was getting harder all the time because they'd eventually be identified and arrested. But when everyone started wearing face masks, even black people after some initial resistance, I wondered if black criminals were maybe just smart enough to see that getting caught on camera hardly mattered when they could no longer be identified—or was I crediting them with more cleverness than they deserve? Maybe they just didn't want to catch Covid while terrorizing, maiming and killing total strangers. Maybe they wanted to kill two birds by protecting their own health while working against the health of others. Who knew what went on in the minds of those mysterious masked villains?

Though the effectiveness of face masks against Covid had been exaggerated from the start, it was their new dual use—disguising and shielding—that was forcing government officials, not just in New York, but around the world to make a compromise. Bans had already been in effect in many places, since long before the pandemic, against face coverings that concealed identities of terrorists and intimidated people in public places. Burqas and niqabs were prohibited, except in religious institutions, from Quebec to Belgium, and these bans were being enforced. Likewise in the U.S., where the Ku Klux Klan's 'hoodies' had been outlawed in many places since the mid-20th century. But now there was no choice but to make an unhappy exception for the masks being worn, at least in theory, to protect public health. Covid made disguises a familiar feature in public squares everywhere, however great the risk to public safety. Across the U.S., crime soared and criminals often got away unidentified. It was not until August of 2022, when Covid concerns had waned in the U.S., that a store in Los Angeles, one of the countless businesses beleaguered by repeated robberies, was at long last able to drop its mask mandate, even to prohibit masks to discourage further thefts and make customers and staff feel safer. The lingering Covid neurotics, and masked bandits, were politely asked to take their business elsewhere.[1]

The choice between public health and public safety need not have been so difficult as made out to be. But Covid-19, the "novel" virus, arrived on the heels of a virulent new strain of "progressive" politics. Responses to both the pandemic and black crime were based on some questionable theory and suspicious motives, often contradicting a wealth of known data and even common sense. Black crime was a simple fact of life, always had been, to anyone with eyes open to tall tales about a nonexistent epidemic of police brutality. It was only to be expected, given their vastly disproportionate contribution to crime, for blacks to come face-to-face with police more often than most people did. Add a tendency to resist arrest, and comparing police to "slave catchers" for defending themselves hardly seemed fair.[2] But in recent years, talking about the ongoing reality of black crime had become more than a faux pas in places like New York where inconvenient truths were grounds for social exile and job termination. The Twitter mob awaited the slightest slipup from anyone who dared question Black Lives Matter's claim that innocent blacks just minding their own business were daily targets of "racist" police, and of the "racist" society that had hired them, so the story went, to oppress blacks—as though police, and society, had nothing better to do with their time.

Before it became a similar heresy to suggest that maybe we were overdoing it with those face masks, scientists openly and matter-of-factly reminded us of what had also been known for some time about airborne viruses. Masking could provide some added safety against Covid infection or spread, though it should have gone without saying that wearing masks outdoors, except in crowded settings, was just plain pointless.[3] Then one day Anderson Cooper, who lives a couple blocks from me in Greenwich Village, was assailed by the press and social media after being photographed riding his bike with a naked face, and suddenly everyone was screaming at me for doing the same.[4]

Popular consensus, I could have told my many militant masked critics from the start and spared them from smelling so much of their own bad breath, had always been to my mind something to resist, especially when based on scant evidence. Mob beliefs, in my experience, were almost always wrong. "They say it was so hot downtown this afternoon," said Al Pacino's character in *Glengarry Glen Ross*, "grown men on the street corner were going up to cops, begging the cops to shoot them … But I subscribe to the law of contrary public opinion. If everyone thinks one thing, then I say bet the other way."[5] For many months of pandemic paranoia and mass mask hysteria, the Covid crazies wasted volumes of bad breath screaming at me with wild, furious eyes made more intense and expressive, like the eyes of silent movie characters, with their mouths covered. Unconvinced of the need to mask up outdoors on my bike, I peddled by sans mask and told them, with a broad and visible grin, to get their minds out of the gutter, to keep their uneducated opinions, and their hot air, to themselves. My antisocial attitude was not well received, and while Anderson Cooper could no longer be easily identified by the paparazzi on his bike, cries of self-righteous indignation followed me everywhere I rode.

From the time of lockdown in March of 2020, mob rules on how to travel, if at all, in public places seemed to change as often as the rules for politically correct speech about black people, which I was also proud to flout. Many of my friends and neighbors would soon become my enemies. Two months of confusion, fear, and general nastiness later, along came the first mass demonstration in New York City over the death of a black career criminal named George Floyd, and with it the chance for my very vocal pro-mask critics to demonstrate how committed they really were to their high-minded ideas on preserving public health.

The overblown claims of a cult called Black

Lives Matter were one thing. How could anyone, whatever their political views, possibly reconcile mass demonstrations with public health *in the midst of a global pandemic?* These protests were more massive than any I'd seen in my forty years of living in the Village, a stage that generations of activists had used to express themselves and achieve "visibility" in the press, permanently parked by our doorsteps and eager for stories to catch on camera and get the world fired up over. The Village still rested on its bohemian past, and seasoned extremists and overnight activists alike came from near and far to voice their frustrations. They united with local college kiddies in their boredom with lockdown living and eagerness to break free from restrictions. They also needed a good leg stretching so long as the gyms were closed. The target of their rage really could have been just about anything, but a ready-made cult like Black Lives Matter, with its prefabricated slogans like "FIGHT THE POLICE," "FUCK THE POLICE," AND "DEFUND THE POLICE," was the perfect excuse for getting out—just after they'd been advised, by the same authorities telling them to mask up everywhere they went, to shelter in place.

Would their flimsy face coverings keep them from catching and spreading Covid while fighting against the sinister forces of white supremacy? It didn't take a medical expert to see that the kind of close, unavoidable contact in these overcrowded, throbbing processions, the long periods of marching and standing side by side, face-to-face, breathing heavily in the hot sun, yelling and spitting anti-cop slogans—these gatherings were surely more risky than the usual "superspreader" events, the weddings, funerals, and other high-risk activities being condemned and banned at the time. It should have been painfully obvious that Black Lives Matter fervor was creating an ideal setting for Covid transmission on a statistically significant scale, a more perfect, controlled environment than the best laboratory tests on social distancing and masking. But "progressives" across the country did anything they could to justify using Americans as guinea pigs in a health experiment for a questionable cause. Our own Mayor de Blasio—I called him de Blackio— magically resolved any dilemma by simply downplaying the disease and calling "racism" a threat to public health, conflating the two but giving Black Lives Matter mania the right-of-way. The pandemic was colored with race, and city streets became veritable Petri dishes for the virus to grow.

I shall never forget the first wave of them, the new "social justice" superspreaders, to come pouring by the tens of thousands down West Fourth Street like a flash flood in the Grand Canyon, lapping at the front entrance to my apartment building while whooshing below my fire escape, five floors up, where I would sit, above the rabble, looking down on them for months to come. The face masks in those early days of the disease were mainly pale blue, but from my high vantage, amidst this sea of disguises, it was easy to make out a preponderance of white people in a mob only peppered, here and there, with black faces. Some of the most wealthy, worldly and sophisticated white people on the planet, many of whom I knew, lived in my neighborhood. All they needed to become international heroes in the war against "racist" cops was to press a button in an elevator, or travel down a few flights of stairs, and head to the street from their ten-thousand-a-month studios or multi-million-dollar townhouses and condos. It was radicalism made easy, and as convenient for any aspiring social justice warrior as having Amazon and Fresh Direct leave daily war rations in their lobbies while they were out fighting whiteness.

The rest of the radical-chic whites, I learned from occasional conversations on the street, had come from Upstate and surrounding areas to show they were just as up-to-date on the latest fashionable causes as those city snobs always stealing the limelight. Mainly-white demonstrators seemed never to stop flowing beneath my window, day and night, with their token blacks, their signs and T-shirts bearing a clenched black fist, the now familiar logo for Black Lives Matter, and the cartoon face of their martyr, George Floyd, who had energized the "resistance" by resisting arrest. Many of the demonstrators who passed below my window could be seen on the evening news as rioters down the road.

We will likely never know to what extent the melodramatized death of yet another black career criminal contributed to Covid deaths in New York City, across the country, and around the world where George Floyd fever spread like wildfire, though science, and common sense, say this surely did help to spread the virus. The chaos and confusion—and the political opportunities—were too distracting for any sensible public health policy at the time. My masked neighbors, those most educated and sophisticated people on the planet, when they weren't performing heartfelt *mea culpas* for the collective sin of "racism"—as confessors during the Black Plague, centuries earlier, took to the streets believing they must have done something wrong to deserve such a punishment—they switched course, and instead of blaming themselves for this divine retribution, sanitized their hands of the matter and scapegoated police for a social problem. Amidst solemn prostrations and wild accusations, lootings and torchings, the chance for a balance between public health and public safety was missed in New York City where the de Blackio administration only added to my dismay by announcing hundreds of workers had been hired for a hopeful Covid "test and trace" program, but that contact tracers were specifically instructed not to ask anyone testing positive if they had recently attended a Black Lives Matter gathering. "Let's be clear about something," chimed in Mark Levine, head of the City Council's so-called "health" committee, "If there is a spike in coronavirus cases in the next two weeks, don't blame the protesters. Blame racism."[6]

As usual, "racism" would be their explanation for everything under the sun.

Weeks later, the press could wait no longer to triumphantly proclaim the results of these health experiments on innocent civilians. The hasty conclusion from much of the media was that protests had caused no "spike" in Covid infections. But the public was being misled by the wording, just as it was misled to believe there had been an epidemic of police shootings of unarmed black men in the first place. Covid surges in other cities were in fact being directly linked to similarly misguided responses to the death of a larger-than-life figure named George Floyd, and it was very unlikely, to anyone with the slightest capacity for skepticism, that performers in New York's street theatrics were miraculously masked against an aggressive airborne virus.[7] Rather, the lack of an *overall* "spike" was attributed, by the more scrupulous sources, to a rise in stay-at-home behavior—among people like me, perched high on my fire escape where the madness could not reach—a wise move when hordes were descending on the city, a strategy that likely offset an overall increase in cases. But by no means did this mean these massive street gatherings had not helped to further spread the virus. Another possible explanation for a failure of Covid to "spike" was that demonstrators tended to be young, and young people were less likely to be counted because they typically had less severe symptoms that weren't noticed.[8] But again, this did not mean Black Lives Matter mania had not helped to spread Covid infections or cause deaths in New York City, or anywhere George Floyd fanaticism was catching.

And what about the many thousands of day-tripper activists who returned to their hometowns Upstate and beyond, infecting their neighbors and grandmothers? Below my window, superspreaders from near and far stayed anonymous behind those righteous masks. They wore them in solidarity with the masked black criminals hitting the streets with newfound boldness, a coming terror they did not see because they still could not accept even the existence of black crime, much less the wildly disproportionate contribution of blacks to crime across the nation that made everyone, white, black, or whatever, *need to hire so many cops in the first place!*

Rather than open their eyes to inconvenient truths, my educated and sophisticated neighbors dressed themselves in contraptions that grew more elaborate and expensive each day. Soon they'd be taking to the streets behind elegant Victorian floral prints and jet-black jacquards, sumptuous silks and satins lined with multiple layers for extra overcautiousness, personalized to fit their individual lifestyles and to balance comfort, filtration and breathability. The Covid virus, like "racism," they believed, was everywhere they went, floating through the air, hiding in the merest nooks and crannies, ready to pop out and infect anyone with their mask, or their "intersectional" guard, down. Their mission was to find and ferret out these twin evils everywhere they went, to expose them to the light of day.[9]

Far from having an enlightening effect, the new fanaticism cast a stifling shroud of darkness all around us. One afternoon, in between mass demonstrations, I walked around the Village I'd known most of my life, now a war zone. Everywhere I went were broken glass, spray-painted stencil images of angry black fists, "Black Lives Matter" murals painted on plywood protecting storefronts, the smell of smoke from trash cans set afire. Police were standing by, but were understandably hesitant to do much. As in those misleading viral video segments shown out of context, anything they did would be used as further proof of what "fascists" they were. If they stopped looters, especially black ones, they'd be caught on camera oppressing the poor. If they arrested raving rich college kiddies setting things on fire, they were caught on camera reenacting the Kent State massacre. When they gathered in line formation and full riot gear, shields up as the mob approached calling for their deaths, they were seen as agents of the military-industrial complex. Many times I risked my life by walking up with my dogs to say hello to society's scapegoats, thanking the working-class men and women in blue, people of all races and ethnicities and one of the most diverse groups I had ever seen, for being there. I asked them if they needed water or anything. They smiled at me and my dogs. They seemed to appreciate knowing not everyone was trying to dump black crime on their heads.

Many of my neighbors (including those who had absconded to their country homes in the Hamptons, Connecticut, and Martha's Vineyard to do their resisting remotely) seemed to revel in the violence, destruction, and lawlessness. To them, this was an exciting chance to be part of history. I shall never forget the swill that came from their mouths in those disturbing, anything-goes times, or see them in a flattering light ever again. Walking up Sixth Avenue, I came upon a wealthy white heiress I knew on Eleventh Street. She was growing impatient with a white homeless man she had always tried to treat as an equal. He'd 'lived' on her corner for years, and locals like her felt better about themselves after leaving table scraps for *their* homeless man. But he hadn't attended an Ivy League school, none of their sophistication seemed to have rubbed off on him, and now he was begging to be politically-corrected. When he expressed dismay over the gang of young people he'd just seen breaking the windows of a nearby bank (where she perhaps collected her monthly trust fund allowance?), the heiress fired back at him through her Burberry vintage plaid cotton face mask: "They're fighting white power!" Here was further proof, in her mind, of how insidious "racism" really was. When it wasn't white supremacist cops, or anyone who wasn't "progressive," it was white supremacist homeless guys. She adjusted her mask and moved on to help fight white power.

I walked a bit further to 13th Street where another ultra-privileged person was also lecturing someone less fortunate. "Why don't you just give me a hundred tickets?!!!!" a white male college kiddie screamed, through his BLM hipster face mask bearing the hand-painted image of a black fist, at a parking enforcement officer ticketing his tiny electric car that was parked illegally. To the rebel with a dubious cause, anyone wearing a blue uniform, even a meter maid, was the enemy of the people and all that was good. The officer, a small Asian man, was only doing his job. He stood silently and took quite a scolding from the baby-faced anti-fascist who ripped the slip of paper from his hand and jumped into his toy car, storming off in a huff along with his token black male friend. Oh, how I wished that cop would have given that college kiddie the beating his parents never gave him. I would have gladly looked the other way, maybe even joined in.

These sorts of scenes were happening everywhere I went. A few blocks away, a gang of militant young Park Avenue heirs and heiresses were planning to take their fight for the lives of black career criminals a step further than hissy fitting. True to a long tradition among rich kids of coming downtown to be rebellious before settling into their fortunes and leading more staid lives uptown, they rented an opulent loft on Broadway they planned to use for an aerial assault on police passing on the street below—until someone informed the authorities and they were all arrested.

When radical-chic social justice warriors weren't out in their stylish face masks punishing police for society's ills, they were at home camouflaging themselves on social media. The latest thing was to change thumbnail profile pictures from actual faces to fields of solid black, a show of solidarity against the nonexistent epidemic of police shootings of unarmed blacks.[10] These were the same people who, a couple years earlier, had transformed their public images into pink, white, and pale blue stripes in support of "transgender" toilets, a show of solidarity against a nonexistent epidemic of assaults on drag queens in public restrooms. How little they had learned. I couldn't resist pointing out something problematic in their latest makeover. "Changing your profile pics to black?" I asked. "Isn't this a form of virtual blackface?" Indeed, it was, though I lost many Facebook friends who didn't see it that way. To them, a white male dog walker was just another white person who was in denial about his privilege and didn't understand "the black experience." No, I had to confess, I did not understand "the black experience," no better than they, or the blacks out marching for Black Lives Matter, understood "the black experience."

While the masked mob went on denying the existence of black crime and crucifying cops for doing their jobs to stop it, harsh reality was creeping into their comfort zone. The outside agitators eventually went back to their less exciting lives in small towns Upstate and beyond to do their part in spreading the virus along with their tales of police brutality. The gyms reopened in the city and the college kiddies no longer needed an activity. My more established neighbors retreated to their townhouses and luxury high-rise apartments to work remotely and order puppies online. The passing mob still kept me up all night but its tone darkened, and in more ways than one. Beneath my window passed downsized flash mobs, distinctly darker skinned, often entirely black. Their chant of "No justice! No peace!" was clearly a threat to anyone who got in their way. They sometimes splintered off from processions to accost or attack customers sitting in those depressing plywood restaurant and café extensions, standard features of the grim new Covid landscape in a town that increasingly resembled a shantytown.

A native of Detroit, I had no illusions about black crime. I had spent forty years in New York, most of these in the Village. I had survived the brutal 80s with firsthand knowledge of the muggings, the wildings, and so much savagery. I had also managed to emerge from the pre-Giuliani years of the early 90s alive, if not unscathed.

But never before had I seen anything like this. Tourists uptown in Times Square, when they weren't being shot by stray bullets, were being stalked and attacked regularly, and by the usual "suspects."[11] To look at the streets downtown in the Village, my neighborhood had in many ways become, and must have seemed to any visiting tourist, a black neighborhood, or perhaps a prison yard. I knew my "progressive" neighbors had been pushing for greater "diversity" and "inclusion," though I doubted this was what they had in mind. Every block had a dozen or more black men, many of them recently released from prison or mental wards, camping out or wandering aimlessly. Some had been set free from the Rikers Island jail complex due to Covid concerns. Adding to their numbers were the repeat offenders repeatedly set free since New York's "bail reform" act had gone into effect a couple months before Covid hit, making this a perfect storm of mayhem. It was sometimes hard to distinguish my new neighbors from the Black Lives Matter demonstrators. My new neighbors shouted at passersby, at each other, at the air, all day and all night. Many had makeshift weapons, like the young black man I passed daily who sat on my corner stabbing sheets of cardboard with a box cutter, over and over, as if practicing for flesh and bone. Many of them, I knew very well, had guns and knives. I was threatened, cornered, attacked daily, as were so many others on my block. Some mornings, it was difficult to step out my front door. "I could smack the shit out-ta you and the cops won't do nothin'," said one large black man while grabbing and shaking me one day as I passed walking a small dog. He was right. My new neighbors knew that even if they were arrested, they'd be back on the street within hours to terrorize again. More times than I can remember, I had to dial 911, like the morning a black man, swinging a metal pipe at me as I passed on my bike, missed and then ran into a store, forcing everyone to run out into the street. More times than I can remember, I had to dial 911 because a black guy was randomly chasing a woman down my block, forcing her to take refuge in one of the shops. More times than I care to recall, I had to dial 911 when a black man, or a black woman, was threatening a Korean shop owner, as they'd done for as long as I'd lived in New York. The police response was always impressive, but the next day these same blacks were back on my block making me dial 911 again. The police must have been as demoralized as I was.

While most of the media tried to ignore or downplay the complete breakdown of a society, a few outlets didn't shy away from the truth. This madness went on for over two years, and the truth only got worse. In 2020, since my new neighbors had started moved in, felony assaults skyrocketed in the Sixth Precinct. By the summer of 2022, the Village, miraculously spared a "spike" in Covid despite having hosted so many mass demonstrations, had the dubious honor of enjoying an 80% spike in felony crimes, the largest increase of any precinct in the city. Since the overblown response to the melodramatized death of yet another black career criminal resisting arrest, robberies were up 42% in the Village, rapes were up 43%, car thefts were up 39%, grand larcenies were up 100%, burglaries (of stores, and of houses left by rich people who'd fled to their country homes to fight white power on Zoom) were up 119%.[12] And all because the gung-ho followers of a mindless cult called Black Lives Matter, intoxicated by a rush of righteousness, had taken to the streets without knowing much about the issues or the side they were espousing—leaving police understandably gun-shy about doing their jobs when they might be shown on camera, out of context, 'oppressing' another innocent black person.

The party was over. Now it was time to pay.

So whenever my radical-chic neighbors, who'd helped bring this hell down upon us all, got randomly pummelled by black men and ended up in the hospital, or when black men robbed them, or tried to run away with their bratty children, I took a perverse pleasure in seeing that for once they had to pick up the tab for their frivolity. *This* was what I called social justice. My glee only grew with the knowledge that, however many terrible things happened to them and theirs, they were powerless to speak up about black crime, or even acknowledge its existence. They would have to grin and bear it from behind their face masks, constant reminders to gag themselves. Calling things by their proper names would get them labeled "racist" and could devastate them socially and professionally. People were being fired on the spot for blowing off steam, like one neighbor who had the impudence to speak up about the sad state of the Village. An agent for a very opulent real estate developer—the kind that had increased homelessness across the city by turning black neighborhoods white—he committed the sin of mentioning how "dangerous" the Village had become. It went without saying that even the word "safe," when used to describe a desirable property, was now a "racist" term, and anyone employing it would no longer be employable.

Unmasked and easy to identify and follow home, I did nothing to pretend I approved of my new neighbors, or that going out for groceries, or walking my dogs, wasn't putting my life in the hands of any number of violent black men I passed every step of the way. I made no effort to play their game, unlike so many of my old neighbors who went through the motions of being welcoming and still living in a civilized society. Any politeness on those mean streets was a disguise. A simple "Good morning," or some other icebreaker like "That's a cute dog," from one of my new neighbors was, in reality, a challenge, a threat to stop and engage in a conversation inevitably leading to a request, in the guise of an aside, for a couple dollars, or possibly face a higher price. I was a notoriously bad neighbor. I kept walking without a kind word in reply, hoping for the best while "I guess you don't like black people!" was shouted repeatedly from behind my back. I was deliberately rude and dismissive, a capital offense in places my new neighbors used to call home. Somehow, I managed to survive their politeness.

The best my radical-chic white neighbors could do was to walk about on tiptoe, struggling to keep up appearances, going through the motions of treating our new neighbors as their equals. The nightmare dropped upon the Village might have been a rare opportunity for them to unlearn their sentimental educations on black crime, to understand what, exactly, it was that police were up against every day of the year, to fill in the missing context to those viral videos with their newly acquired, firsthand knowledge—to face directly what black people themselves endured their whole lives in their own neighborhoods but "progressives" didn't allow each other to even talk about in theirs. If "black crime" was a redundant expression, "black-on-black crime" was doubly redundant, and as my neighborhood got blacker, black neighborhoods became death traps. But instead of using a valuable life experience to improve themselves, each time my "progressive" neighbors were threatened, robbed, or attacked, or when they witnessed others falling random prey to our new neighbors, they mumbled, under their breath from behind their face masks but close enough for me to hear:

"The police never do *anything*."

There it was. The same people who, with their street theatrics and careless embrace of a cult called Black Lives Matter, had joined to tie the hands of law enforcement across the country, the ones who'd shouted to "defund the police" and fanned the fury that got police harassed, scorned, humiliated, maimed and killed for supposedly doing too much to confront black crime—were now complaining that police did not do enough.

I went about my daily business, leaving to someone else the burden of being "inclusive" of the characters lining my sidewalks. It wasn't that I didn't *like* black people, however much I had come to loathe my white neighbors. It was just that I was *bored* with black people. For months, I was kept up all night by the drone of "No justice! No peace!" It grew louder after a moron named Jacob Blake left police no choice but to shoot his dumb ass.[13] I'd seen it all before, starting in 2014 with a thug named Michael Brown who while shoplifting attacked the immigrant shopkeeper, then attacked a police officer and tried to take his gun, and not surprisingly, also got his dumb ass shot, and killed.[14] It was always the same scenario, over and over and over. I saw my city transformed into a monotonous war zone, lines of businesses boarded as far as I could see, angry black fists everywhere I turned, murals to black hagiography, statues to George Floyd. In the years leading up to this full-scale infatuation with blackness, I saw movies with token black actors inserted awkwardly and unbelievably. I avoided all the absurd, pandering remakes with all-black casts. I saw bookstores with entire walls devoted to predictable titles on "racism" that flooded the market. A trip to Barnes and Noble, once it reopened after Covid shutdowns, was like going to an ice cream parlor to find the only flavored being served was chocolate.

Much like the inflated portrayals of police shootings that had gotten everyone into a hoopla in the first place, the closer and more real black crime became during Covid, the farther the media went in the opposite direction to show black people in a wildly flattering light. I travelled two parallel universes, one real, the other virtual. While people in my city and across the country—white, black, or whatever—were being terrorized and savaged, the media engaged in black overkill to

the point that it was impossible to read a magazine, turn on a television, or log on to the internet
without entering a world where virtually everyone
was black. A black guy in an expensive suit bought
his girlfriend expensive jewelry. A black family in
chinos jumped into a luxury car and took a drive
in the country. A black woman came home from
work, not to do someone else's laundry, but to
shake her bootay around her sleek, modern apartment while doing a quick load in her new LG
WashTower. A white woman sang hip hop and
danced black around hers. A black skateboarder
with Zulu hair gave his imprimatur to the latest
bacon burger. The Metropolitan Opera made opera less white by adding jazz. This had passed a
saturation point. "Visibility" had gone too far. It
seemed every essay, article and film offered me a
chance to learn about "the black experience," in
case I hadn't learned enough. Every channel had
a chorus of "Black Voices" supposed to teach me
something I didn't already know.

A couple blocks from my apartment, in
Washington Square Park, blackness had become
especially tedious. Everywhere I looked were
groups of black men, huddled together whisper-

ing, dealing drugs, doing drugs, asking for free money. They didn't wear chinos, but whatever they had managed to find on the street. They were allowed to occupy the park for many months, and despite widespread violence, including rapes. The police were told, in so many words, not to interfere. Community meetings, in church basements around the Village, were shouting matches between white people fed up with the crime and squalor, and other white people screaming "Racist!" at them for not appreciating these representatives of a different "culture" who had, they claimed, as much right to use a public park as anyone else.

One afternoon I needed to cross Washington Square in a hurry and pick up a dog I was scheduled to walk. I might have gone around the park, but time was short and I had to cut across diagonally and take a walkway I had affectionately started calling "Crack Alley." Sitting on benches that lined the path on both sides were black men and black women, one after the other, sitting in a stupor, or passed out across the benches. Rushing through as quickly as possible, I sensed a presence coming up from behind to my left. A well-dressed black woman, perhaps an employee of New York University which bordered the park, was also in a hurry to get through its creepiest patch. Unlike my radical-chic neighbors, she was not afraid to describe what she saw.

"Blowing crack in broad daylight???!!!" she shouted as one of the black men exhaled a cloud of smoke our way then covered his mouth again with a face mask.

"What is this, 111th and Lenox???!!!" she added in an exasperated tone, referring to an infamous corner in Harlem, as we increased our clip and passed neck and neck through the gauntlet of toxic air coming at us from both sides. For once, I wished I had a face mask.

We both managed to get through Crack Alley unharmed, emerging near the center of the park where the fountain sprayed as usual and the arch framed the vista up Fifth Avenue.

"I have to *live* here," I said to the well-dressed black woman. She stopped and gave me a big smile, then kept walking.

She got my joke.

ENDNOTES

1 Salvador Hernandez, "The surprising reason why this L.A. boutique says it banned COVID masks: Crime," *Los Angeles Times*, August 23, 2022, https://www.latimes.com/california/story/2022-08-23/l-a-kitson-boutique-bans-covid-19-masks-citing-crime.

2 Heather Mac Donald, "Blue Truth Matters," *The American Mind*, September 21, 2020, https://americanmind.org/features/ending-the-blm-revolution/blue-truth-matters/.

3 John Tierney, "Approximately Zero," *City Journal*, February 17, 2023, https://www.city-journal.org/new-cochrane-study-on-masks-and-covid; Nie, Kang, Pian, Hu, "Need for more robust research in preventing COVID-19 transmission," *Future Medicine*, April 19, 2022, https://www.futuremedicine.com/doi/10.2217/fvl-2021-0032; Marc Silver, "Should we be wearing masks outside again?," National Public Radio, January 22, 2022, https://www.npr.org/2022/01/22/1075049518/should-we-be-wearing-masks-outside-again; Klompas, Morris, Sinclair, Pearson, Shenoy, "Universal Masking in Hospitals in the Covid-19 Era," *New England Journal of Medicine*, April, 1, 2020, https://www.nejm.org/doi/full/10.1056/nejmp2006372.

4 Deirdre Simonds, "Anderson Cooper goes maskless on a bike ride through the city as New York's

number of coronavirus cases jumps to a whopping 102,683," *Daily Mail*, April 3, 2020, https://www.dailymail.co.uk/tvshowbiz/article-8186607/Anderson-Cooper-goes-maskless-bike-ride-city-number-New-Yorks-spikes-102-863.html.

5 *Glengarry Glen Ross*, TM & © Lionsgate (1992).

6 Tobias Hoonhout, "De Blasio Tells Covid Contact Tracers Not to Ask Positive Cases If They've Attended BLM Protests," *National Review*, June 15, 2020, https://www.nationalreview.com/news/de-blasio-tells-covid-contract-tracers-not-to-ask-positive-cases-if-theyve-attended-blm-protests/.

7 Randall Valentine, "Relationship of George Floyd protests to increases in COVID-19 cases using event study methodology," *Journal of Public Health*, August 5, 2020, https://academic.oup.com/jpubhealth/article/42/4/696/5880636.

8 Dave, Friedson, Matsuzawa, Sabia, Safford, "Black Lives Matter Protests, Social Distancing, and COVID-19," Cato Institute, "Research Briefs in Economic Policy," October 14, 2020, https://www.cato.org/research-briefs-economic-policy/black-lives-matter-protests-social-distancing-covid-19.

9 Michael Brandow, "This 'racism' thing," *Medium*, October 9, 2019, https://medium.com/@michaelbrandow/this-racism-thing-e1bad68ab36b.

10 Heather Mac Donald, "There Is No Epidemic of Racist Police Shootings," *National Review*, July 31,

2019, https://www.nationalreview.com/2019/07/white-cops-dont-commit-more-shootings/.

11 Michelle Acevedo and Dennis Romero, "4-year-old girl, two women shot in New York's Times Square," NBC News, May 9, 2021, https://www.nbcnews.com/news/us-news/toddler-woman-shot-new-york-s-times-square-police-say-n1266765; Kimberly Richardson, "Times Square shooting: 23-year-old woman shot during chaos thought she'd never see daughter again," Eyewitness News, May 9, 2021, https://abc7ny.com/times-square-shooting-nyc-wendy-magrinat-tourist/10603908/; Myles Miller, Jonathan Dienst, "2nd Times Square Bystander Shot in Broad Daylight in 2 Months, Mayor Vows More Cops," NBC New York, June 28, 2021, https://www.nbcnewyork.com/news/local/police-search-for-shooter-who-injured-tourist-walking-with-family-in-times-square/3127758/; "NYPD beefing up Times Square police presence after Marine shot," Eyewitness News, June 29, 2021, https://abc7ny.com/times-square-shooting-today-man-shot-in-nyc-new-york-city/10839150/; Brittany Kriegstein, "Panic in Times Square as dozens flee from possible gun shot," *New York Daily News*, August 29, 2021, https://www.nydailynews.com/new-york/nyc-crime/ny-times-square-costumed-character-hurt-panic-20210829-xwmoyivoxvgeffco2mi5aq2tvq-story.html.

12 Andrea Grymes, "New NYPD statistics show shocking crime increase in Manhattan's 6th Pre-

cinct," CBS New York, August 18, 2022, https://www.cbsnews.com/newyork/news/new-nypd-statistics-show-shocking-crime-increase-in-manhattans-6th-precinct/.

13 Brittany Bernstein, "DOJ Won't Pursue Charges Against Officer Who Shot Jacob Blake," *National Review*, October 8, 2021, https://www.nationalreview.com/news/doj-wont-pursue-charges-against-officer-who-shot-jacob-blake/.

14 Doug Wyllie, "Why Officer Darren Wilson wasn't indicted," Police1, November 24, 2014, https://www.police1.com/ferguson/articles/why-officer-darren-wilson-wasnt-indicted-b3DTG-pEkDemKS2P5/.

ABOUT THE AUTHOR

Michael Brandow writes on society, the arts, and canine culture. The author of several books on subjects ranging from public policy to social history, memoir, and political commentary, he has contributed to many publications including the *New York Times*, the *New York Post*, and the *Village Voice*. A sought-after commentator, he has spoken to radio audiences around the world. His works have been listed in *The Best American Essays* and he has been profiled in *The New Yorker's* "Talk of the Town."

Ingram Content Group UK Ltd.
Milton Keynes UK
UKHW021837230523
422237UK00010B/143

9 781943 003846